FEAR TO FIRE

FEAR TO FIRE

MY LIFE
AS AN AIDS ORPHAN

Stephanie D. Castagnier

iUniverse, Inc.
New York Bloomington

FEAR TO FIRE
My Life as an AIDS Orphan

iUniverse books may be ordered through booksellers or by contacting:

iUniverse
1663 Liberty Drive
Bloomington, IN 47403
www.iuniverse.com
1-800-Authors (1-800-288-4677)

Because of the dynamic nature of the Internet, any Web addresses or links contained in this book may have changed since publication and may no longer be valid.

ISBN: 978-0-595-43304-9 (sc)
ISBN: 978-0-595-87644-0 (ebk)

Printed in the United States of America

iUniverse rev. date: 10/21/2010

This book is dedicated to the loving memory of the two most beautiful, inspiring and influential people in my life. Mom and Dad, this is for you. I love you.

Margaret Sugrue (1959–1992) and Richard Castagnier (1956–2000), your legacy lives on.

I would like to thank my family, friends, and everyone who has helped me through the good and the bad. I am forever grateful.

Contents

THE COLD OF WINTER

On December 14, 1992 at the young age of thirty-three, AIDS stole my mother's life. It was a cold and gray winter day in Montreal. The air was stale and the winter sleet messily splashed the parked cars and sidewalks. The city was dirty and depressed. I was sore from months of crying and sleep deprivation. Most of all, I was defeated. The one person I loved the most had been taken from me that morning. I slowly made my way back to our dark house after the funeral. There was no need to rush home that afternoon. No one would be there waiting for me in the kitchen. No family dinner was being prepared for us that evening. I walked through our front door without purpose and without hope. I went through what little remained in our abandoned house and came across an envelope taped under a shelf in Mom's bookcase.

Mom loved to write and had secretly written excerpts about her life. She had taped them under a shelf in a small bookcase in the hallway. She last worked on her manuscript several months prior to her death. I found it by accident as I cleared the books she kept. I have decided this story is too important to be left untold. Her writings are included in this book as I continue with my story. Mom wrote about her life; her love, her regrets, her anguish, Dad, Grandpa, our family, and me.

Mom was taken from this cruel world defeated. Our story has conjured many questions. Should family interfere in domestic violence? Do we have a responsibility to help our brothers, sisters, grandchildren, nieces and nephews? Where does responsibility start and where does it end? Should you say something to someone walking into a fire or too close to a dangerous ledge? My loss has led me to question our human responsibility.

HOW DID WE GET HERE?

Dad let himself in. He snuck through the front door trying not to make a sound, like a thief in the dead of night. Mom and I were both asleep. At least we both pretended to be asleep. We had become so accustomed to these nighttime disturbances that we slept lightly. Dad tiptoed down the hall and headed straight for the hallway closet. He hoped something valuable would suddenly appear that was not there an hour ago. Mom lay still in her bed and I did not dare make a sound. This must have been the fifth time that night that Dad had come in and the fifth night in a row that week. Actually, Dad had been playing this game for the last two or three years.

The trick was to pretend we were asleep and pray he would have pity on us and not want to wake us. If he knew either one of us was awake, he would ask us for money. Dad continued to forage moving from the hallway closet to the kitchen; where he looted the cupboards. Then, he moved into to the bathroom; where he searched the medicine cabinets. By then, he had turned on all the lights and knew we had to be awake. He was looking for something, anything he could sell to get money. He went straight for one of our usual and few hiding places; bottoms of drawers or deep in the closet corners. We hid anything we could. Money, winter coats, shoes, jeans, alarm clocks and anything else that could be sold.

Tonight, he could not find anything worth selling. Four times a week over three years, there was hardly anything left in the house at all! Not a radio, piece of jewelry or piece of clothing worth more than five bucks.

"Well, she got paid today, so she must be hiding it somewhere" we could hear him murmur to himself as he savagely tore through the cabinets.

Then I saw their bedroom light flick on down the hall and knew exactly what was coming.

"Gimme twenty bucks Nancy!" at first he whispered pretending to care if he woke me.

"Gimme twenty bucks, hurry I have a cab outside waiting for me, gimme twenty bucks."

He had a coarse voice when he came home stoned. It sounded like he had sand in his mouth and desperately needed a drink of water. The smell of his breathe was disgustingly peculiar and, unfortunately, very familiar to me. Even now, years later, I would be able to tell you what that smell was. His breath smelled sweet which made me nauseous only because I knew what he had been doing. It was the smell of crack, blood, booze and filth. He would push himself in your face, spit and sweat all over you to get what he wanted; money.

No matter how familiar we were with this frequent routine, we would always try to fight back.

"Are you crazy?" Mom cried out "Get the hell out of here, I'm not giving you a penny. Every time you come in you take something else. Forget it, get lost!"

She cried out pretending to be brave but Dad saw right through to the fear in her eyes. You could hear a tremble in her voice as she belted out. My door was open and I could see them down the hall. The light from the hall blazed into my room and my eyes burned from being wakened so many times that night. My head pounded and I was just tired of it all. Tired of life and tired of this crazy world.

"Gimme twenty bucks or I'll take your coat. Don't make me take it," he threatened. It was mid-December and freezing in Montreal this time of year.

"I just bought that coat, you sold my old one and I have no money left to buy another one! Please Richard!" Mom sobbed backed at him.

"I paid your mother the rent today and bought food, something you never do, so leave us alone."

Dad knew she had to give in now. "Gimme twenty bucks and I won't come back tonight, I swear."

Mom looked away and did not respond.

"Well, if that's how you want to be, enjoy your walk to work tomorrow morning." Dad grabbed Mom's new coat from its hiding place, under her summer shorts in her drawer, and stormed out the front door.

"You damn junkie, I hate you!" Mom yelled after him as he quietly closed the door behind him. I felt relieved that he had not come into my room this time but this meant next time would be my turn. Mom had nothing more to give him tonight. It was always a negotiation game with him and we never won.

The quiet after the storm was an empty chilling feeling. We both felt defeated, tired, depressed and alone. The house was still and we lay in our beds eyes, filled with tears but just tired of crying all the time. We both hid our tears as not to upset one another any more than we already were. I never wanted her to know I heard the whole fiasco so I pretended to be asleep most of the time. She knew I had to be awake with all the commotion going on only a few feet away.

Commotion she did not want me to worry about. So I lay still and listened for her to turn the lights off and console our dog Corey.

"Daddy's gone now Corey, go back to sleep, everything is OK." Mom cuddled with Corey in her bed and they both tried to go back to sleep. It wasn't so easy to fall back asleep after those events. My heart thumped for an hour and I cried for about fifteen minutes. I prayed to God to make this all stop. I prayed that my father would realize the pain he was causing us and suddenly change. I also prayed that God would just burn down this evil house so we could move away. We felt like captives in this hell and there was no way out. This was our routine, three to four times a week, several times each night. I never really got any sleep during my early teens. This night had not been too bad. He was fairly calm because he got what he wanted. We did not always have things to give him so he would become desperate and violent. He would push us around, shove us into the walls, throw things at the walls or punch holes in the doors. Dad had been a boxer when he was younger and was still very fit. When he punched the wall, you could feel the blow in the pit of your stomach. We were extremely afraid when he became violent and desperate because he did not know his own strength. He would pull my arm to see what I was hiding behind my back and almost break it! I lay stiff in my bed every night thinking, "How are we going to get out of this? If he doesn't kill himself, he is going to kill us. How did we get here?"

The rickety alarm clock shrilled half heartedly; it was an old beat up clock. Dad had sold their electric alarm clock some time ago. This old alarm clock was not worth more than a buck so it was spared.

"Steph, time to get up dear, its seven o'clock," she whispered stroking my hair. "Is the idiot home yet?" were usually my first words in the morning. "I heard him all night coming in and out," I said angrily. "No, your father is still out, get up now," Mom replied emotionless.

She went to the kitchen to prepare our lunches.

I walked into the kitchen rubbing my eyes asking, "What did he get this time? I heard you arguing about your new coat, did he take it?" I asked in a disappointing tone.

"Yup, he did, it's gone so don't worry about it." "Well what are you going to wear to work? It's freezing outside," I asked. "Don't worry, I'll wear a few sweaters," Mom reassured me. "I can't believe you let him take it? Why didn't you hide it better?" I was upset and fed up. "You didn't hide it well enough," I repeated to myself.

Mom answered back calmly, "I'm tired of hiding everything, besides, there are no more hiding places left and what's the use? He just finds it and we all get upset for nothing."

I felt tired, angry, frustrated, and defenseless in the morning. I could just imagine how Mom felt. Her only wish was for us to lead a normal life. Instead, we were trapped in this nightmare. We were alone but at least we had each other.

THE EARLY YEARS— DOWNTOWN LIVING

Thinking back on my childhood, I feel as though I am from a completely different world. I can't believe I have survived and continued living after all the danger and pain we experienced. My memories and experiences are unlike those I hear my friends share. It is as though my life has been one big dream or nightmare. One in which I am just hoping to wake up. I have been waiting for the perfect time in my life to sit down and write my story. As events throughout my life have unfolded, I have stored each of them deep down and concentrated on getting through each day. I guess that is how I have gotten this far. I try not to think about anything that went on around me and have focused on just worrying about the small daily issues.

The reason I have always wanted to share my story is to give hope and inspiration to others who may be living similar experiences. Growing up, I never knew who to turn to because I felt no one would ever understand. I felt as though no one really cared because they all had their own problems to deal with. I also felt no one said or did anything because they didn't know how to help or what to say. I kept all my anger, insecurities and fears to myself; until today.

I grew up in downtown Montreal at 3820 Sewell Street. We were near the corner of St-Laurent and Pine Avenue, a very posh and hip place today. It was the slums back then. My father wanted to live downtown because that was where the "action was" he said. We moved there when I was five years old, right before Elementary school. My Dad bought a duplex with my grandfather and grandpa renovated it himself. Dad always told me he bought the duplex but to this day, grandma says she bought it. Who knows? Everyone always remembers their own version of history. I guess the story is told by those still left to tell it.

They tore down the old building and rebuilt this duplex literally in the heart of the ghetto.

I was fine with the whole move. There were kids next door and up the street. As a kid, I was more interested in making friends than real estate. The area we lived in was predominately Portuguese. My first friend was my neighbor Sandra. We spent the first summer playing elastic and other mindless games. Life was great. I was a typical child without a care in the world. We were all happy.

Dad's business was busy. He was an "entrepreneur" Mom said. Many times at school, teachers would ask what my parents did and I said, "My father is a very successful entrepreneur!" Which was true. He was making millions. We had fancy cars and nice clothes. Dad traveled a lot and we went on family vacations to Florida and Mexico several times a year. I had no idea what Dad's job was then but he was happy and that meant we all were. I was five years old at the time so I didn't really ask questions about Dad's career. Mom stayed out of his business and just took care of me all day. She didn't spend any money; ever. She was very conservative and low key. Always wore the same old clothes and her fashion goal was to draw as little attention to herself as humanly possible. No makeup and no fancy haircuts. She did not like any attention.

Money was never a problem for us. Small bills came in large oversize garbage bags on a weekly basis. The garbage bags lined the basement walls. I would watch Dad in their bedroom counting the money all night long. He would call me over to help him count. He would give me a pile of hundred dollar bills too big for me to hold in my hand. I had to count them in piles of one hundred and put rubber bands around each pile. He owned several businesses; a garage, a laundry mat, a butcher shop, a few night clubs and a few strip clubs. We would drive around with him during the day as he made his "collections" from each business. Mom and I waited in the car most of the time as he ran in. He insisted on bringing us everywhere he went because he said he missed us too much when we weren't around. Mom didn't work so we both followed him around. He had a lot of men working for him everywhere. The "collections" were endless. We drove around the towns of NDG, Ville St-Pierre, LaSalle, and Lachine while he made his quick run-in stops.

That first summer living in the city, we finished up our new house and it looked great. It was the only brand new duplex on the street and we even bought a four person hot tub to put in the basement. The floors were all hard wood and the kitchen was finished in beautiful tile. The kitchen had beautiful wood cabinets that my grandpa worked on all summer. The rooms were all very spacious for downtown living. My bedroom was at the end of the hall beside the kitchen. I had a window which led to a view on the alley. Not much of a view but at least I had a window. I had a pretty bedroom set. It was country white with a book case, dresser and bed. My room was fully decorated with the Strawberry Shortcake collection. From the bedspreads to the curtains, Shortcake was everywhere.

Mom and Dad's room was back down the hall towards the front door, sharing the living room. It was only separated by a half wall on each end.

There was plenty of space for the three of us in our little apartment. That is, the two of us and our black Labrador Corey because Dad was barely ever home.

The best part about living in the city was that my grandma and grandpa Castagnier lived right upstairs. I was so close to my grandma and grandpa that I called them Mami and Papi. I loved having them so close and so did Mom. Mom and Mami were always together and were the best of friends. While I was at school all day, Mom ran errands with Mami and they drank tea every afternoon. My grandfather, Papi, worked for a Jewish family in Westmont. He did construction work and other maintenance projects for them. They owned several buildings and a hotel downtown which Mami managed. Before living downtown, we lived in Lachine in an apartment. Mami and Papi lived in NDG, in one of the Fleming's buildings where Mami was the landlord. Mom worked back then for the town of Westmount as a clerk. While Mom was at work, Mami would babysit. Every day, I followed Mami around while she did her daily janitorial duties. She would scrub the floors on her hands and knees and I would watch. I loved spending time with her. I remember the basement well in that old city building. It was very dark and had the old basement mold smell to it. It was scary down there but Mami was never afraid. She was a strong and fierce woman and nothing could scare her. She was a tough little lady. She would stick her two hands in the boiling water bucket, dipping her mop and not even make a sound. I would ask how come it did not hurt her hands and she replied that she didn't feel a thing. I guess she had a really high paid threshold. She stood about five foot four with dark curly hair and spoke English with a thick French Canadian accent. I would speak to her in English and she usually replied with a mixture of French and English. She was a no-nonsense woman with a job to do and would do her job to the best of her ability. I probably learned my work ethic at an early age from her. She was very disciplined and never complained about anything. She accepted her place in the world and proudly did the job she was paid to do.

REVOLVING AROUND ME

Life as I knew it, revolved around me for both Mom and Mami. Well, that was how it felt to me anyway. I attended St. Patrick's elementary Catholic School a couple of blocks away from our street. Mom would walk me to school every morning, pick me up for lunch, bring me back to school and pick me up again at the end of the day. I ate half a sandwich and a cup of soup every day for lunch and as soon as the Flint Stones TV show was over, it was time to go back to school. St. Pat's was a very religious school with prayer sessions every morning before school began. The school itself was new and clean and we were even served breakfast every morning after prayers. They would serve warm oatmeal cookies, cereal or cheese with a small carton of milk. The highlight of my life was when it was cookie day. I lived for the cookie day. I joined the choir my first year in elementary school because I was always very interested in music. Our choir was very well known in Montreal. We recorded a record, played at the Christmas concerts at Ogilvy's department store, and sang on the radio. Every year we sang for a televised event, The Telethon of Stars. Mom and Mami stayed home glued to the TV to tape every performance. I began taking piano lessons and quickly became accustomed to being ahead of the other kids musically.

My cousin Melanie was the first one in the family to take piano lessons. The first time I saw her piano and heard her tap at the notes, I knew I just had to play. I begged Mom and Dad to let me take lessons. My first couple of years learning to play I studied at a small music school in Westmount on Sherbrooke Street. My teacher was a fat little lady who was friendly and jovial. I don't remember her name today but I guess she kept me interested. I was a soprano singer in the choir and loved music. I continued on with my piano lessons once we moved into the city with a teacher a few blocks away from Sewell. Her name was Linda and she was extremely gifted. I took lessons with Linda until I was seventeen years old, when I just didn't have the time or the money anymore because of school and all the moving around. My biggest achievement was attaining Level eight with Honors at the Royal Conservatory of Music. An accomplishment my parents would have prized dearly after over a decade of investing in my talent.

I was also a very active swimmer at a very young age. Mom began taking me to swimming lessons and the YMCA when I was about four. After we moved to the city, Mom found a local pool up the street on St-Laurent call Schubert Pool where she signed me up to continue my lessons. Schubert Pool was very old, actually a historical landmark. It had stone walls and ceramic flooring in the entrance hall and had grand stairs at the door up to the pool area. There were stained glass windows all the way up the stairs. It was very beautiful and bright. Upstairs was dark and had a very strong chlorine smell. I guess they needed high doses of chlorine for the downtown pest infested clientele. Mom would bring me to my lessons three times a week and sit there through the entire lesson watching me attentively and waiving back when I yelled, "Look at this Mom!" Mami came often with Mom and they kept each other company. I had my own little fan club; my very own entourage all at the young age of six. I can't remember even once looking up to the stand not to see Mom sitting there looking right at me with an adoring smile. She never even brought a book to read or do anything else but watch me. There was really nothing spectacular about watching a six year old trying to swim laps, flapping around in the water. But she loved every minute of it and I felt like I was on top of the world.

She always made me feel as though I was the best at whatever I was doing. She was the proudest mother in the world. I, however, can't remember a single time when I saw Dad sitting there with her. We had grown accustomed to life without him but for some reason I always knew he was close by, somewhere. We just never talked about him or where he was. Mom made sure to keep me busy so I never even had time to wonder where he was all the time. I assumed he was on an important business trip somewhere. Mom probably liked the distraction of keeping busy with me so she didn't have time to worry about Dad. She never commented about Dad in a negative way for not being around.

WHERE WAS DAD?

As I grew older, I began to wonder where Dad was all the time. Where was he and what was he doing all day long? Mom worked hard at keeping me so busy with school, choir, swimming, piano, and playing with my friends and cousins that we were always running to some appointment. My best friend was Sandra. She lived on the second floor in a duplex across the alley from my bedroom window. I met her in the park across the street one day and we played together everyday from that day forward. We went to the same school and she even took swimming lessons with me. She was Portuguese but did not like the other Portuguese girls in the neighborhood. She said all they did was gossip all day and she did not want to be mean like them. So it was an upset to the other Portuguese girls that she and I were such close friends. When we were eight, Sandra's family decided to move back to Portugal. I was so sad but too busy with my busy schedule to worry about it. My daily routine went on and I was good at everything and soon became the best at every activity I did.

My only purpose in life was to make Mom and Dad proud. I was always the top student of my class, never had a grade below ninety. I won every race I swam in and always brought home a medal for Dad to hear about. After Sandra moved back to Portugal, Dad disappeared for a while. I found out, years later, that he had served a two year sentence at Penn State Penitentiary or some prison out there for drug dealing in the U.S. He was busted for a really big drug transportation some- where in New York. At the age of seven, my perception of time was altered. I knew Dad was away for some time but it never felt like two years. He had become such a small part of my daily life that I barely even noticed he was gone. I do remember writing letters to Dad all the time and he would write back to me. Mom said he was away working and everyone went along with it. He would send me little ceramic beer mugs and jewelry boxes he made himself and wrote "I LOVE YOU STEPH" on them and signed his name. Mom probably deliberately kept me busy so I did not have time to realize what Dad was up too. Maybe this was her way of getting out of the house and out of that mess Dad was spurring.

In the summer before fourth grade, Sandra moved back to Montreal from Portugal! Her family decided to move back and it was as though they had never left.

The rest of my years in elementary school were OK I guess. I graduated from elementary school with the highest grades in the class. I continued with piano lessons and was now playing some impressive pieces. I also continued with swimming three to four times a week. One day, while I was playing with Sandra in the park, Dad appeared over the bushes walking up Clark Street. This dark, strange man yelled out "Steph!" and I looked over not knowing at first who it was. Sandra asked, "Who's that?" and I replied "It's my Dad!" running over to him with tears in my eyes. He looked different since the last time I saw him. His head was shaved and he was very big and muscular. He was an impressive sight. I jumped into his strong arms thinking to myself, "It's my Dad and I love him!" The three of us crossed the street and walked over to our door. Mom and Mami were sitting in the kitchen sipping on tea as usual. Everyone was ecstatic to see him and life as I knew it with Dad started that day for me.

THE TUNNEL

After Dad came back from prison we began going on frequent vacations again as a family. Dad was determined to make up for lost time away from his family and wanted to get to know us again. We went out for dinner often, just the three of us. That year, we went to Mexico for a three week vacation. Dad had a friend who lived there and one of my Dad's cousins came along. I think it was that year, when I was about ten or eleven that I began to pay more attention to Dad's business. His lifestyle and behavior had always been normal to me because it was all I had ever known. To me, this life we led was normal and for all I knew, everyone's Dad brought a garbage bag of money home at the end of the day.

We definitely were doing well up until this point. Dad drove a Mercedes and Mom a brand new Monte Carlo which she absolutely loved. Dad had two or three Harleys in the backyard and we traveled all, the time. We traveled more than anyone else I knew. We had been to Florida about five times, to Mexico for three weeks and even drove across Canada in our van Dad had bought. We stopped in every capital of every province from Quebec to B.C. It took us two weeks to cross the country. Throughout the trip, Dad would constantly call home for updates on his businesses. We stopped to swim in the hot springs in Banff when Dad found out one of his Harleys had been stolen. His cousin was in charge of everything while we were gone, so Dad was furious when his cousin told him the bike had been stolen. No one should have stolen that bike. It was in a closed yard and everyone in the neighborhood knew it was my Dad's. He was not someone anyone would want to steal from. Dad suspected his cousin from the very instant he told him but never said a word to anyone but us. That was the end of our escapade. Dad rushed us back into the van and we drove back non-stop to Montreal for him to sort out his affairs. It took us four days to get back to Montreal from Vancouver. Dad never trusted that cousin again with anything.

Dad kept in great shape and taught me that being physically fit was very important. He taught me how to box and made me do sit-ups and push-ups every day. He would always tell me, "Steph, a healthy body is a healthy mind and you have to be strong to survive. You have to respect your body and work hard at keeping it in shape." We had fun going to the McGill University campus track where he would run along side me; backwards to push me to run faster. Dad reminded me a lot of a Rocky type character. Fun, thoughtful, and a strong fighter at everything he did. Sandra would come along most of the time. I always had friends over for dinner. All my friends loved Dad because he made everyone feel like they were family. He played with us for hours; joining in board games and cooking for us all. Dad made the best home fries you could ever imagine. He would have boot camp where he taught all the neighborhood kids to box and to exercise. I had little boyfriends when I was young and they all loved to come over to hang out with my Dad! He was fun and interesting. He could converse with just about anyone. He loved to get to know people and to talk about life. I was proud to have a cool Dad that everyone wished they could have. He was my Dad and my best friend. I could tell him anything. He was just cool and understood the things we faced in school. He shared similar stories about bullies and mean teachers. He just understood me, he understood everyone.

Dad had a difficult childhood. He was born of French Canadian parents in a small depressed town called Lachute. He had an older sister, Darlene, older brother Jacky and a younger brother Gary. The extended family was also extremely close and everyone lived in the same town. Papi was a construction worker from a poor family. Mami was also from a poor family of fourteen. Both sides of Dad's parents were from traditional French Canadian families. The more kids you had, the more help on the farm and a "more direct route into heaven," so the parish priest explained. The Church's way of keeping the Parish prospering was to encourage reproduction! Dad grew up very close to his brothers, sister and cousins. Dad was the most loyal person you could ever meet. He loved his family and would do anything for them.

Aunt Darlene took care of Dad growing up. She would help him get ready in the morning for school. Dad had so much trouble in school. He was illiterate but the teachers, at that time, thought he was just being hard headed. The teachers said he refused to learn and Dad would be sent home from school every day with his head hung low and tears flowing down his cheeks. He did not understand why school was so difficult for him when everyone around him seemed to understand what was being taught. He wanted to listen and understand what the teacher was teaching but it just did not register. Every day, Dad knew his mother would be waiting for him at the front door with a leather strap in her hand. Years later, the family realized that Dad was dyslexic and could not have possibly learned in the fast paced regular classroom. He would have needed special attention.

Thirty years ago, schools did not explore learning disabilities. Everyone just assumed it was disobedience and the child needed to be punished with physical discipline. Every day, after school, Dad's mother tried to beat intelligence into him as hard as she possibly could. Dad told me stories about his mother doing mean things to him and beating him viciously. It was hard to imagine Mami being so mean but I believed every word Dad said. Dad said that Mami was a different person when she was young. He said she was sick back then and today he had for- given her. Dad never did learn how to read or write. He barely got by writing his own name. The beatings made him physically tough and he eventually became a boxer. He turned to what he was good at, fighting.

Dad was a really good boxer. He won every fight he was in and was proud of his abilities. He had found an activity he enjoyed and finally something he could excel in. He took pride in his abilities and thought he could make a career out of his talent. Dad had talent and a passion to win. He was convinced he would become a world champion. He fought with the famous "world of boxing" Hilton brothers and said he could even beat them. At the time, the Hilton brothers were the fighters to beat. Dad trained with them and followed their career paths. Mami eventually said it was too scary for her to watch and forbade my father to box. She was too afraid he would get hurt so she forced him to stop. Since Dad was not yet eighteen years old, he needed parental consent. Mami would not sign the consent form so Dad was forced to stop participating in the sport. He always resented her for that. His love for boxing continued but his desire to come back into the sport a few years later died as he discovered a more profitable pastime.

With his strength, passion, power and charisma, Dad turned to the other ventures he was good at, making money dealing drugs. He was the most popular guy in town. He was good looking, strong, fit, and everyone listened to him. Probably because he could be mean if you were not on his good side, so people were afraid of him. He made you feel as though you were his only friend in the world and was always there for you. He made good money fast and could never walk away from easy money. Every business he tried worked and he made money doing anything. He had the "golden touch" his friends said. He started off small and local. Everyone in town was involved in the business and he was the boss. He made all the decisions and told everyone what to do in the organization. He just knew how it was all going to work and exactly what steps needed to be taken. Everyone knew about his business activities and admired him. No on had ever seen that kind of money where they were from. Dad was a great businessman. People loved to work for him because he took care of his employees. Everyone made money and he was always fair. He was also loyal and defended those who worked with him. If you had Richard on your side, you were protected and respected. He had the world in the palm of his hands and he was only eighteen!

When he was eighteen, he met my Mother. Mom was a student at Mary Mount high school and they had mutual friends. They were introduced and

Dad said it was love at first sight. He said Mom was different. She did not approach him and she was shy. Dad asked who the shy girl was. Mom was not interested in money or power so she did not pay any attention to him. This of course motivated Dad; finally, a conquest. They started seeing each other more and more at parties and around town. Eventually they started dating. Mami told Mom that my Dad was sterile and could not get her pregnant. Big help that was because, sure enough, after months of unprotected sex, Mom was pregnant! Mom was sixteen and Dad was eighteen when they were faced with this big decision. Here is Mom's account of her beginning with Dad, found after her death among her writings:

> Life with Richard had never been easy. When we first met, I was only fifteen years old and Richard, the Mr. Cool of the Montreal neighborhood in NDG. He was a hothead eighteen year old. After an evening together, he would drop me off at home at 10:00 PM and then hit the streets. Whatever the gang was up to, Richard was usually the leader. Even at eighteen, he had a powerful love of money and control. He was also a friend to everyone. He influenced people easily but was also manipulated himself. He and his gang of delinquents would roam the neighborhood, breaking into houses or stores, stealing car radios or bicycles. Richard started drinking and smoking pot and hash very young. Then, when he saw what kind of money could be made in the drug trade, he soon started dealing drugs. He started small, selling grams of pot and hits of acid at Rock shows downtown. The Montreal Forum and the streets of NDG were his stomping ground.
>
> I knew about some of Richard's business and thefts, but didn't take it too seriously. After all, when I was with Richard, everyone treated me like I was someone special. I felt honored that king pin Richard had chosen me to be his girlfriend. "I like you because you're different" he told me one night sitting under the stars in the NDG park. "You're not like all those other girls." "What do you mean those other girls?" I asked blushing. "I've gone out with a lot of girls around NDG and they are douches, turn your back and they fool around with your best friend. But I trust you. You are shy and quiet and smart." I felt warm and happy wrapped in Richard's arms. I could overlook all those terrible things he did, anyways I rationalized, he knew what he was doing and he was making money, wasn't he!
>
> So, as innocent as puppy love can be, this was the beginning of their lives together. It is hard for me to imagine them in love years later as I look back at our lives. There was a time when they did feel love and happiness.   Reading this, from my mother after

she died, I now know that they did have love for one another in the beginning.

In winter of 1986, things at home started to change for us. Papi Castagnier was diagnosed with cancer. He fell really sick very fast. Before we all knew it, Papi was bed ridden and dying. Papi was only fifty-nine and Dad definitely took it the hardest. We had never seen Papi weak and vulnerable. He was a tall and impressive man. He cried when any of us were around and it tore us all up inside. Mom wrote this in her manuscript titled "The Tunnel" about Papi's experience with cancer:

I watched as my father-in-law, Armand Castagnier, struggled to get out of his car. He was coughing so hard, it was no easy task. It was a cold, damp afternoon in December. Freezing rain was pouring down, soaking everything, leaving lakes of water everywhere that would later that night, freeze to form miniature skating rinks. I was hiding under the awning, trying not to get wet as he came up the walk.

"Hi," he said between hacks. "Are you OK?" I asked him. "Yeah, Yeah I'm alright," he wheezed and he waved his hand at me to dismiss my concern. "I was just going upstairs too," I said. He climbed heavily up the stairs in front of me to the second floor flat that he shared with his wife, my mother-in-law, Jeanne. The warmer air in the house helped to stifle his cough.

His daughter Darlene, a tiny dark haired girl, was visiting with her husband and two kids.

"Hi Pa, do you still have that cough? Why don't you go see a doctor? You've had that cough for weeks and it isn't getting any better." She said as her father walked into the kitchen.

"Yes Armand," his wife Jeanne agreed, "We could go to the emergency clinic tonight, you might have an infection in your lungs."

Jeanne was a hard working, feisty, French Canadian lady who has raised four kids with Armand. She is a short, plump, dark haired woman with oversized glasses covering her tiny brown eyes.

"They're right you know, it could help to see a doctor Dad." I said.

"OK, OK, I'll go to the bloody hospital, you women love to nag," he chuckled "I am fed up with this cough, maybe they could give me something good for it."

Right after supper we all rushed off, I live downstairs from my in-laws with my husband Richard and my daughter Stephanie so I didn't have to go far. We didn't want him to have any excuse not to go. Armand was notorious for his negative attitude about doctors. "They don't know their ass from their elbows" he would comment whenever anyone had a story to tell about an unusual visit to the doctor. A combination of fear and mistrust had kept him from any regular visits to the doctor. He had to be really sick to go see one, which is how he must have felt because he didn't resist much that night.

"Good, I'm glad," said Darlene, "I've been worried about you, I'll be relieved when you have a check-up."

Later that night, around eleven, I heard them get home. The staircase of the duplex is inside the building so I always hear when people come and go upstairs. So I telephoned them to see what had happened. Jeanne answered, "Hello."

"Hi Ma, how did it go, what did the doctor say?"

"Well the doctor thinks he may have pneumonia, so they took some lung x-rays and they will call when they have the results." She said.

"Pneumonia! You're kidding, boy, he really is sick."

"They're not sure; it could just be a bad cold. Armand wasn't too happy, we waited over two hours to be seen, so he was crabbing as usual," she said.

"The doctor said he has all the symptoms, fatigue, fever, night sweats, shortness of breath, cough, but we'll just have to wait for the results."

Armand was told to take a few days off work but being the stubborn man that he was, he didn't last at home long. By the second day, he was back at work.

Armand Castagnier was a jack-of-all-trades, a handy man for an investment company that owned a group of buildings all over Montreal. Some days he was painting offices, other days he would be doing carpentry, and others repairing a furnace. He had been at his present job for twenty-five years but before that he had done a lot of things, mostly house painting and factory work. He would say, "God gave me two hands and two legs to work hard, so I'll never worry about making a living."

He loved to work; when he wasn't working at his job, he was working on one of the duplexes he and his wife had bought. They renovated the two places completely from ripping out the old walls and floors to installing new heating, plumbing, and electric wiring. Most of the work he did himself. He was very good at it and his wife and kids were proud of him but were always after him to stop working so hard. He had also built a chalet up north, doing almost all that too. He had three sons Jacky, Richard, and Gary, who had helped him with his places. All his four children and their husband and wives loved him and respected him enormously.

He was also a French Canadian like his wife. He was of medium build with premature white hair, which was slicked back with water and a comb in a kind of James Dean style. The premature white really bothered him, to the point where he would let his wife put Miss Clairol rinses into his hair. In an attempt to restore his hair to its natural dirty blond, she achieved all different hues, from a brassy yellow to an auburn tinged gold. His kids would tease him about the dye jobs and he would blame it on their mother. He was partially deaf in one ear so you had to raise your voice to speak to him. His kids all grew up shouting at their father so they learned to speak loudly even to each other. When the whole family gathered together, the sound level during a conversation would be at an incredible roar.

He was famous for his big nose. That was the first feature that anyone noticed about him, he came from a long line of big noses, and all his brothers had also inherited that giant honker. He had incredible light blue eyes that contrasted with his dark complexion. He was a striking, good looking, and impressive man.

Jeanne called his work the day the results came in. She should have and could have waited until that night to tell Armand what the doctor said when he called, but she was so shook up; she told me later, that she had to call.

The receptionist at his job took the message that he was needed at home right away. Armand took it as an emergency and rushed home.

"What, what is wrong, what happened?" he shouted as he came in the door.

"Calm down nothing happened, the doctor called with the results so I wanted to tell you," Jeanne answered.

"God, you scared the shit out of me, I thought you were sick or hurt, why did you tell the office it was an emergency?" he asked annoyed.

"I didn't say it was an emergency, I said it was important and it is," she said quietly, "the doctor said they found something on your x-rays."

'What's wrong with the x-ray, oh my God, they found something bad!"

"It could be nothing," she said quickly trying to reassure her worried husband, "It could be a mistake or maybe it is pneumonia, don't panic."

"Don't panic, it could be a tumor or cancer, God, please, no, it can't be," cried Armand.

"They need to take more tests to see what it is, meanwhile try not to worry," she said.

When the news got around the family, we were all scared. There was a family history of lung cancer, Armand had already lost two brothers to the disease.

The next few weeks were filled with tests, x-rays, blood tests, and specialists. Armand and Jeanne were always asking questions, they were anxious and needed answers but the doctors were reluctant to give any. So Armand went home each day frustrated and more uneasy. Assuming the doctors were indif- ferent to his case, he became angry and resentful. The waiting for results became unbearable and every night, some of the family would gather together at their father's home trying to ease the tension.

Finally, the long awaited results came in and the Castagniers went to hear the verdict. When the doctor announced his news, it was such a shock that he told Armand and Jeanne to go home and let the news sink in and he would see them again in a week or so to plan their line of attack against the disease. I heard the terrible news that same day.

"I can't believe it, are they sure?" I asked Ma. "It's definitely cancer?" "They're sure, they are talking about chemotherapy and treatments and we are so confused," she said. "I don't know what to do, what do you think, should I start these things?" asked Armand. "I really don't know Dad," I stammered, "It's got to be your decision." "I just can't give up without a fight," he said, "the doctor said a lot of these treatments are experimental and I don't want to be a guinea pig." "Well, what did the doctor say if you don't take the treatment?" I asked. "He said I have a tumor the size of a peach inside my lung and it could be attached to my esophagus or the other lung so it is inoperable, but he said not untreatable. God, I can't believe this crap, cancer, why me, I still can't believe it's true," he said, his voice breaking.

"Of course you have a choice," said Jeanne, "You don't have to do anything you don't want to do."

"I just can't give up and not fight, I have to do something," he despaired.

"It's all so confusing, we don't understand a lot of what he says, he always talks in English," Jeanne said.

"I'll go with you if you want Ma," I offered, "When you hear more about these treatments, maybe you'll be less upset. They have been having a lot of good results with some of these ideas."

That first appointment I attended with my in-laws was like a dream sequence. It felt as if we were discussing someone else's sickness, a stranger's disease and treatment. Dad was calm and listening carefully to every word. The doctor was specific, it was a fast growing cancer and treatment was to begin immediately. If they didn't, Armand wouldn't have much time. At the Royal Victoria Hospital, there were several treatments available for different cancers but for this type, the recognized approach was chemotherapy and radiation. The doctors were experimenting to see which combination of the two was more successful. Chemo or radiation first? There were two study groups, one which received the standard way, chemo first and radiation second and the other group received the reverse. Armand had his choice of which group he would like to be in.

"I really don't know, which method works better?" he asked the doctor.

"We still don't know that ourselves, it's a new study and we haven't got any reliable result yet," said the doctor sympathetically to all of us, "I'll leave you alone to discuss it and you can decide if you want to proceed with the treatment."

He left us alone in a tiny white office, I felt very awkward.

"Well, I don't think you should accept this chemo, he said himself he didn't know if it would work," said Jeanne.

"I think it sounds worth a try, he said if I start right away they could shrink this damn thing. I don't have much choice, do I? I have to try." he said hopeful.

When the doctor returned, he was glad that Armand had decided to join the program and he proceeded to tell us all about the chemotherapy and the side effects. He also told us that the most important factors to a patients' recovery were positive attitude, good morale and keeping in good health. That meant maintaining a good diet, and getting lots of rest. The next decision was which study group Armand wanted to be in.

"I'll let you decide, Doctor," he said.

"OK we'll put you in the group which needs additional participants, how's that, and we'll get started as soon as possible," the doctor said with a warm smile. He put his arm around Armand's shoulder as he walked us out.

A couple of weeks later the treatments started. Chemo would come first followed by radiation. Armand told me he was relieved because this was the standard way they had been treating people with lung cancer. Chemotherapy is a procedure in which they inject massive doses of powerful drugs into the blood stream in hopes of killing the cancer cells and therefore, shrinking the tumor or at least arresting the growth of new cancer cells. But as the poisonous drugs are intruding into the patient's system, they are not only killing cancer cells, they are also causing a toxic reaction inside your body.

I was at the hospital when Dad had his first treatment, he was visibly trembling but smiling and talking with the nurse as she hooked up the intravenous, which would facilitate the numerous drug injections he would have that day. The drug she started with was a dark red liquid in a little plastic hanging bag. It was so potent that the case had to be taken out softly so as not to let any drip or leak onto the patient's skin because it would cause a burn. Myself, I was shivering with fear and tears filled my eyes as I watched this brave man trying to combat an invisible enemy, the disease that was literally eating him up inside.

Mom and I stayed with him for the first couple of hours, and then we went outside to get some air. This ordeal was hard on her too, to watch as the man you've been married to for over twenty-five years faces the unknown, and to share that unknown with him.

That first treatment was to begin a pattern which the Castagniers would face for the next six months. One day of injections followed by three or four days of weakness. The toxic chemicals were poison to his body, and caused unbearable sickness. Then the hair loss began. Little by little ,Dad watched his thick white hair fall out. We all joked and teased him good naturedly so he wouldn't take it too badly. His sons started buying him caps, which he took to wearing everywhere to hide the hair loss.

During this time, Darlene and the boys tried to be supportive and spend a lot of time with their father. The fear and pain they were feeling themselves, buried beneath a smile and a laugh.

The doctors assured Armand that the treatments seemed to be working but that nothing was conclusive yet.

One week in early summer, Armand had a respite from the onslaught and decided he wanted all his family gathered together up north at the chalet, that coming weekend. It was a summons that we couldn't refuse. We spread the word among us that we all must be present, no exceptions, so everyone assem- bled Friday night at the chalet near Mont Laurier. It's a big four bedroom place in a Swiss chalet style; it was crowded with us all there.

It was a beautiful weekend; the weather was warm and sunny. The lake was calm and the water rippled softly from the light breeze that blew. Armand, from an old lawn chair on the front gallery, watched his grandchildren play in the yard beside the lake; he had tears flowing down his cheeks.

He looked happy then, thinner, balding, but healthy and content.

We were sorry to go home on Sunday, I wished we could have all stayed there forever; safe, harmonious, and peaceful but reality returned for Dad Monday morning, more treatments and more sickness.

When the first round of chemo was over, they started to give radiation therapy to Armand. Radiation therapy is a focused x-ray centered on the tumor to try to burn and shrink it away. The side effects were not as bad then. He was tired a lot and his skin burned in the area on his chest where they focused the radiation but his nausea wasn't as bad.

As the months wore on, we all kind of adjusted to his disease. It had become something we lived with and he battled with on a constant basis. I started to believe that maybe we could just go on like this forever. The cancer never leaves, it's always present but you start thinking maybe he won't die; maybe we could go on for year like this. Man is a very adaptable specie.

After the radiation, he was given a rest for a few weeks to recuperate some of his post strength. His doctors would only say that they were happy with his progress, still noncommittal, and that everything looked good. Armand looked well and said he felt great which made us all optimistic.

I spent a lot of time with my in-laws that year, and got to know them both better. They told me stories of their lives together, the good and the bad times they had shared. Dad wanted to spend a lot of time with his children and grandchildren and wanted to share their lives and they all cherished the time they had with him. I know he became a very dear friend to me and he taught me a lot about life and love.

The next appointment was in late September. The doctor was very positive and the news were encouraging.

"Armand, the tumor in your lung has shrunk to a manageable size and we are very optimistic about your future, I'd say you'll be able to go back to work soon and be able to resume a normal life too." The doctor said.

"The tumor is gone, you're kidding, that's incredible! Are you sure?" Dad exclaimed. "Wait, it isn't completely gone but it's about the size of a pea now and we think it's under control for now. I want you to understand that it could start to grow again and we would have to start the treatments over, but for now everything looks good." the doctor said.

"Thank you so much doctor, that's great, I can't believe it," Dad said enthusiastically.

"Thank you, thank God!" Mom said.

"Now, now, I want you to still take it easy, I don't want you to go back to work yet, you still need to rest. We want to keep an eye on you too. We'll schedule an appointment for you to come back to see me in a few months." The doctor said smiling.

So they went back to living their lives, the kids were ecstatic when they heard the good news. It felt like a battle won; it had been a long hard year but Dad had been victorious over the damn disease. Everyone started planning a joyful winter and a spirited Christmas celebration.

Then, a few weeks later, Dad woke up one morning feeling feverish and sore all over. "Maybe I have a cold or a flu coming on," but his voice was anxious.

"Let's make an appointment to see the doctor just to make sure it's nothing," Mom said.

By that evening, the pain had become excruciating. They went the next day to the doctor and the tests began again. The blood test revealed active cancer cells in his system, so they scheduled more tests. Dad went to the hospital for a weeks stay to have a bone marrow aspiration; a very painful procedure where they take a sample of bone marrow for analysis.

I went with Richard to visit his father in the hospital that night before the big test, and we brought a candle we had blessed at St-Joseph's oratory. Armand was a very religious man whose faith greatly helped him through this ordeal. We all prayed for him that night.

He was reluctant to talk about the possibility of the cancer returning, so we tried to keep the conversation light. Everyone came in later and it turned into a melancholic party.

He returned home after the tests to wait again for results; all the while the pains in his back worsened and moved down into his legs.

"What can make me hurt this much?" he moaned to Jeanne. When the answers came, they were devastating. I received a call around six o'clock one evening, we had just finished eating and I was cleaning up the kitchen. Mom and Dad had been home from the hospital for a while now but I was too scared to go see what the doctor had to say.

It was Mom on the line, "Come upstairs with Richard, your father has something to tell you all, I've called the rest to come over too," she said her voice was muffled and strained.

"We'll be right there," I assured her.

I told Richard but he hesitated to go up right away, so did I, but I knew we had to go, we couldn't desert them now. So we climbed the stairs, my heart was pounding, I felt dizzy. I was the first one there, Richard headed for the kitchen, he couldn't face his father yet. Mom couldn't talk. She cried silently and tears ran down her cheeks. Dad was in the living room, sobbing, it was the first time I had seen him cry through all this.

"What is it? What did they say?" I asked.

"They said the cancer has moved into the bones, it has generalized, in the blood, the bones, that's the pain, what the hell, he promised, the doctor promised I would be back to work soon, I'm dying," he sobbed hysterically.

"God no," I whispered.

"What am I going to do? What can I do? I can't start over that damned chemo, I can't take anymore,"

I sat stunned across the room, wanting to reach out to him, but I couldn't, I mumbled something stupid, "It'll be alright, don't cry, you'll be OK."

His children couldn't face him. One by one they arrived and sobbed uncontrollably along with their father. We were all devastated. Mom collected them together in the kitchen, being strong, firmly sitting them down with a cup of tea and quieting the tears. I sat alone in the living room with Dad. He had quieted but he couldn't turn off the tears. They trickled down into the collar of his pajamas. I was so cold. It was freezing in that room. I guess it was just me. I didn't know what to say but I couldn't leave him alone.

"What do you think dying is like?" he asked abruptly, "Do you think there really is a heaven?"

"Heaven, well yes, I think there is a heaven," what do you say to console a cancer victim? I was without words for a few minutes.

"I've heard, and read about, people who claim to have seen a place like heaven," I started quietly, "These people have had near death experiences, they're stories are all a little different but it is weird how they are so similar." Dad was listening intently.

"Yes I've heard shows on the T.V. about that," he said.

"Even the experts can't explain how the stories are so alike. These are people who have been brought back from the edge of death after an accident, heart attack, or such. They almost all said they had the feeling of leaving their bodies floating above and looking down at themselves. Then, they were traveling down a tunnel, at the end of this tunnel was an intense, warm, light and as they traveled down the tunnel they met all the friends and family that had passed away before them. At the end of the tunnel, in the light, is God, well not exactly God but a man they identified as God. The people who have experienced this all say it was very peaceful, warm, and happy and they weren't scared or worried," I told him.

"Do you believe their stories?" he asked. "Yes Dad, I think I do believe them," I assured him softly. He had calmed down now and he smiled. "I'll get you a coffee and something to eat, you must be hungry," I left the room and his daughter Darlene went in to see him. I could hear them both crying loudly.

He refused to take any more treatments; even the doctors agreed there wasn't much use. It would just weaken him and make him miserable. He was prescribed morphine and Mom was told to try to make him comfortable and give him anything he wanted. The liquid brown morphine helped the pain and let him sleep.

He worsened quickly; the cancer ravished his body. He lost weight because the morphine upset his stomach so he couldn't keep any food down.

We would take turns visiting him in the evenings, sitting by his bed. On his really bad days, we would suggest he go to the hospital but he didn't want that. He said he wanted to die at home. Mom respected his wishes but it was hard on her. He wouldn't let anyone else take care of him. She nursed him day and night neglecting her own health. She hardly slept because the pain kept him awake almost all night. She hardly ate anything and she couldn't go out of the house because he was afraid when she went out.

His children found it so hard to sit with him. The proud, strong, stubborn man that had been their father was now a feeble old man.

I went to see him everyday, we talked about all kinds of things. I wanted to believe he would just get better one day and it would stop. We all went through day after day, functioning but not living as before, just waiting.

Instead of the joyful Christmas we had planned, it was a sad time. We went to dinner at the Castagnier's as we always did. Dad wanted us all together one last time, he wanted one last Christmas. Nobody could enjoy any of it, we put on a good act but Dad was so sick by that time he couldn't eat any turkey or visit with the little kids; he suffered terribly and endured the pain quietly. It was a terrible Christmas day.

We continued all to visit him through New Years; he deteriorated fast. By then, he was taking so much morphine that most of the time he slept. When he was awake, he didn't always recognize us. He would hallucinate and sometimes he would just lie in bed and whimper from the pain.

The nurse would come for regular check-ups and give advice but Mom did it all. She bathed him, fed him, encouraged him, nursed him, gave him his medicine, and she was wonderful; I have never seen strength like she displayed.

But even her strength couldn't keep her going. Early in January, she was exhausted, physically and mentally, she was so busy caring for Armand, she had no time to take care for herself. He was so bad now, he cried a lot, was almost always incoherent; it was as if he was completely someone else. He even looked like a stranger. He was a skeleton, so thin you were afraid to help him sit up for fear of breaking his bones. He was ravished with pain; the deep lines were engraved in his face. He was almost completely bald from the treatments he had received and was pale and gaunt.

One night I was at their house with Jacky, my husband, and Gary. The three boys were there because they were worried about their mother.

"Ma, let us take him to the hospital, you can't do it anymore. You're exhausted. Please let us call an ambulance," said Richard.

"No! He wants to die here, at home, in his own bed, not alone in a hospital," she cried.

But you could see she was not sure herself if she could continue.

I said quietly to her, "Ma, let us take him, you are so tired, he won't even realize he's in the hospital, he's so confused now he doesn't even know who we are."

"Do you think so, I don't know." She was crying now.

"OK, just let us take him to the hospital for a few days, we can bring him back here after you've had a rest," Jack said, "Call the ambulance, he's going to the hospital."

"Yes, he's going," agreed Richard.

The ambulance arrived shortly and they tried to talk Mom out of keeping Dad in the house. Her kids knew that this was very hard on her and it had to be. So they took him to the Royal Victoria Hospital (R.V.H.). He never did return home to his own room.

He was in the terminal care unit of the R.V.H. In his final week on earth, he was kept comfortable. The nurses were wonderful, understanding, and sympathetic to the family. There was someone of the family always keeping a watch over him. Day and night, his loved ones stayed by him, they didn't want him to pass away alone.

One day, I was in his room when he gained consciousness, his two sons, Richard and Gary, had just stepped out for a coffee and a cigarette. He opened his eyes and saw me standing there.

"What are you doing here?" he asked.

I was shocked by his voice but said, "I came to visit you, it's me, Nancy, how you do you feel?"

"You came to visit me?" he sounded very confused. The boys had come hurrying back into the room at the sound of his voice. "Daddy, daddy, it's me, Richard, and Gary is here," Richard cried. He held his father's hand tightly in his. We were all crying. Gary said, "Daddy, I'm here too." "I saw Jesus, Ricky, I saw Jesus, he was here for me, and now he's gone."

His voice was joyful and light. We were all so overcome with joy that he could speak to us. It had been so long that he had recognized any of us. "Jesus will be there for me when I go," he said smiling through his tears.

He cried tears of joy. Not long after that, he was asleep again. He was only with us a couple of days after that, again silent and dreamlike, as if in a coma. Armand Castagnier (our father) died on January 13, 1986 at the Royal Victoria Hospital. He was not alone. He was fifty-nine years old. Somehow, as I stood in the funeral parlor and prayed, I knew that our Mr. Castagnier was not on this earth anymore. He had made that journey down the tunnel towards the bright, intense, light and was at peace forever. I still think of my dear friend and father I had loved so dearly whenever I feel lonely or need to feel his love. He will always be close to me, here, in my heart.

(The Tunnel, written by Margaret Sugrue)

After Papi passed away, a part of Dad died with him. As my goal in life had always been to make my parents proud, Dad too had that same desire with his father. When Papi died, Dad always told me he just lost his way. He did not have the strength to fight every day and stay focused. He was mad at the world. He had been very close to his father and could not understand how God could take away the person he loved the most. After the devastating loss of Papi, the fun and inspiring Dad I had grown to love began to fall to pieces. He allowed the loss he felt from the death of his father to begin to destroy him. Dad began to take the drugs he had made so much money selling. He started with just a little; then, he couldn't get enough. He turned to drugs to drown his sorrows and his life quickly spiraled out of control. The wonderful parents I had up to this point in my life were about to change. It is interesting how one event can change everything. Papi's death was the beginning of the end for our little family of three.

Dad was so greatly devastated by the loss of his father that he allowed this loss to change him. He allowed this loss to change him into someone he was never meant to be. He lost his innocence and his will to succeed. It was a slow process but it had been triggered.

To understand how someone can change so drastically overnight, it is imperative to start from the beginning of who they were. As easy as it is to be a good person and do the right thing we are just one wrong decision away from becoming a bad person and doing the wrong thing.

MOM

Mom was born in an English-speaking Canadian family. She was from Irish and British blood. Their family had been in Canada for many generations, over 250 years to be exact; they just considered themselves "Canadians". Anglophones are the English speaking Quebecers. Francophones are predominately French speaking. There is a huge cultural difference between Anglophones and Francophones in Quebec. That is Quebecers who were predominately French speaking and Quebecers who were English speaking. The Anglophones living in Quebec lived in specific anglo neighborhoods and were quiet and conservative. The Francophones focused on family and often gathered together for loud parties. The Francophones are similar to the typical Italian families, where everyone is a major part of the family. Mom's family lived in Hudson, a quiet Anglophone village west of Montreal. When Mom was 11 years old, her family packed up and moved to Montreal to look for work. Mom had an older sister, Maureen, and older brother, Peter. Grandpa Sugrue got a job in Montreal working as a blue collar laborer and Nanny Sugrue worked in an accounting department. Grandpa Sugrue had served in World War II. This granted them permission to live in Benny Farms, an old run down apartment community for Canadian war veterans. It was a dangerous little ghetto in the heart of the city. Nanny Sugrue was very determined and extremely intelligent. Grandpa was an alcoholic and never played an active role in the family. Nanny Sugrue ran the household alone and raised her three children as best she could. Papi spent the majority of his time at the local bar, so money was very tight. They were very poor and lived in a small two bedroom apartment. A family of five living in a two bedroom apartment was crowded to say the least.

Growing up, Mom was the most outgoing of the three children. She was pretty, sweet, and very intelligent. She was always top of her class in school and was always the smart girl in the crowd. Even though she was always top of her class, she did not study much. Instead, she enjoyed spending time with her friends. School was always really easy for her. Through her group of friends at Benny Farm, she met my Dad.

The Mom I knew, after years of fighting the war we lived, became shy, quiet, and spoke only when she had something important to say. She had dirty blond hair and dark green eyes, which hid behind thick dark framed glasses.

She was a very thin girl who never thought much of herself. She believed her best feature was her brain. When she was fifteen, she met my Dad who was unlike anyone she had ever met. At first, Mom was not too impressed but when Dad showed undeniable interest, I guess she was flattered. She was the center of attention and went from being invisible to popular overnight. Mom wanted to get away from her family and the little apartment they all crammed into. Hanging out with Dad was her way of getting a break. Dad's family was fun and had big family parties all this time. Mom became friends with all of Dad's family members and enjoyed the fun family ties she had never experienced.

Mom found out she was pregnant only a few months after they started dating; my Dad who was supposed to be sterile. Her immediate reaction was abortion. Dad said there was "no way in hell that he would allow the child he was never suppose to have be taken from him". Besides, Dad's mother offered to help as much as she could. She even offered that they live with them. So together, at ages sixteen and eighteen, they decided to have this baby; they would figure it all out along the way. Since they had only been dating a few months, they were both excited about this now "very serious relationship."

Mom was graduating high school the year she became pregnant. Breaking the news to her mother was not going to be easy. Nanny Sugrue was excited about Mom graduating from high school and going off to University. No where in Nanny's plans was there a baby for my Mom, at least not this early in the game. Not for the next ten years! Mom told Nanny that she loved this man and was keeping their baby. She assured Nanny that everything was going to work out just fine and that everyone would help. Nanny was hesitant at first. She encouraged Mom to think hard about having an abortion. She believed that mom was too young and throwing her life away. She explained that there was no shame in an abortion; especially at such a young age. But Mom was determined to be responsible and take on the challenge of becoming a mother. She felt strongly about doing the right thing. She felt she had fallen pregnant for a reason and was going to assume the responsibilities of her actions. Timing was not great, actually timing was really bad. But if she became pregnant miraculously with Dad, she quickly convinced herself this must be meant to be. Mom was nervous and uncertain but knew one thing; she could not kill her baby. Nanny Sugrue said she would help as much as should could and accepted her daughter's decision.

Mom left school before the end of the year. She was beginning to show and her school principal pulled her aside one day. He said she was a bad example for the other girls and would prefer that she finished her school year from home. She was not the image the school wanted to portray to the other parents. Her homework was sent home to her on a weekly basis. She felt rejected and lonely. Was she getting herself into something she would regret? Mom ended up graduating from high school that year, but was not permitted to attend the graduation ceremony with all of her friends. Her Diploma was sent to her in the mail several months later. She had gone from being a straight "A" model student all her life to the class reject. This hurt her self-esteem and impacted her confidence level for the rest of her life. She thought less of herself academically because of this humiliation.

At first, Mom and I lived with her family; my Grandma, my Grandpa, her sister and her brother in their small two bedroom apartment. It was now more crowded than ever. There were now five and a half of us living in the tiny two bedroom apartment. Everyone helped with the nightly feedings even though they all still had their own lives to live. Mom felt guilty for subjecting them to the life she had chosen for herself. She could not see my Dad as much as she wanted to so Mom and Dad finally decided to rent an apartment. They rented what they could afford, which was a small apartment in Ville St-Pierre on Windsor Street. This apartment could be compared to living in Cambodia thirty years ago. It was as poor as could be in a crime infested street similar to the Bronx. The young teenage couple, with their newborn baby, started their life together. They always double checked to make sure their front door was locked before going to bed at night.

Mom spent countless nights alone in that apartment while Dad was out building his empire. She would cry for hours because I was a cranky baby who enjoyed endless nights of crying and whining. We both cried all night. Here are Mom's writings found after her death:

> It was New Year's Eve, 1976. In about thirty minutes, a new year would begin. Dick Clark smiled out from the T.V. screen. New Yorkers in Times Square were dancing and screaming and already cheering in the New Year. Sitting in my living room alone, I couldn't look forward to another hour, let alone another year. I had just experienced the hardest year of my life. From the other room, I could hear my baby beginning to wake up; fresh tears sprang to my swollen eyes and trickled down my cheeks.
>
> Six months earlier, on July 2, 1976, at the age of sixteen, I had become a mother. When I first found out that I was pregnant, I couldn't believe it. I was terrified and confused. I didn't know what to do. Telling my boyfriend, Richard, was easy. He was thrilled. He was only eighteen years old, but he was so sure that we were in love and could make a life together and live happily ever
> after, that he had convinced me. But telling my mother was another story; I knew it would break her heart.
>
> "Ma, I have something to tell you," I said one evening when I caught her alone in her room.

"What is it, dear?" she said.

"I don't know how to tell you this, I know you are going to be mad," that was the understatement of the year, I thought.

"Just say it, go ahead," she said, smiling. "Well. Well. I'm pregnant," I stuttered. "You're PREGNANT. No, I can't believe it, are you sure? After everything I've told you. And after you swore that you and Richard were not even having sex. I could kill you. I should make you have it that would be your punishment, to have to raise it." She exploded. "What are you going to do now? Go for an abortion?"

"Ma, I've already talked to Richard and he wants us to move in together and raise this baby together, I'm not sure if I'm going for an abortion." I said. My mother's voice softened "But you are only sixteen years old. How will you raise a child? You are still a kid yourself. What about college and your own future? Think about this before you decide. It's a big responsibility raising a child, think seriously about it. If you don't want to have this baby, I will understand. An abortion may be the best thing. I can't help you much; you know that, I have to work too. I can't stay home and raise your baby."

"I know, and I wouldn't expect you to. I will think about it." I assured her. "I have time; the doctor said I'm only a few weeks pregnant."

I thought hard about it and with Richard and his family's supportive and helpful advice, I decided to keep my baby.

During my pregnancy, I experienced feelings of isolation. While I tried to dismiss these feelings as silly, I felt a change coming. My friends treated me differently by excluding me from the group. They were supportive but aloof, caught up in their own adolescent world.

Of course, I spent most of my time with Richard. We daydreamed about the great life we would live. Richard had found a full time job and was already saving a little money for our future. I was still attending my last year in high school. Luckily, it was the year of the Olympics in Montreal so I would be graduating in May instead of June. I thought I would be able to attend the graduation ceremony as I wouldn't be too big by that time and the grad gown would hide the pregnancy. I was terribly hurt when the school principal asked me not to attend. I also had to write my final exams in a private office away from the other students. I assume so I wouldn't be an embarrassment to the faculty and administration.

But I graduated and received my diploma from the same principal. Two months later my daughter, Stephanie Dawn, was born. The delivery was a nightmare. I had a fever of 102 degrees and red spots all over my body. The hospital staff never did diagnose what it was I had; they decided it must have been a virus. The labor pains were incredible. Nothing that I had been told could have prepared me for them. But after eight hours, I came through in one piece. My daughter was quickly whisked away and placed in an incubator. I wasn't allowed to hold her because of the spots, which I found ridiculous since I had carried her for nine months. She'd already been exposed to anything I had. Richard took off for an all night celebration with his family.

I was lying awake in my lonely hospital room worrying about my baby. Where was she? Where had they taken her? What if she needed me? What if she got sick and they didn't take care of her. I couldn't even remember what she looked like. I had only seen her for two minutes through the glass of an incubator before they took her away. I cried myself to sleep.

Three days later, I was finally released. All the spots had disappeared and the fever was gone. I had spent all three days in isolation and hadn't seen my baby at all.

When they presented her to me, my heart leapt. She was so beautiful. She had great big eyes and pale blond hair. I examined her tiny face and hands.

"What are these pimples all over her face?" I asked the nurse. "Why does she have these blue marks over her eyes?" I was sure she had been mistreated by the nurses.

"Those are just bruises from the forceps the doctor used during delivery, and the pimples will go away. They are normal on a newborn, don't worry, she'll be fine in a couple of days." The nurse assured me, smiling.

So, after a few short instructions on feeding, I was sent out into the world with this new little life to take care of. I was terrified.

At first, I went home with my family. My brother and sister were enchanted with the baby. They cooed at her and examined her for hours. My mother was sweet and kind. After my final decision to keep my baby, she completely supported me. She bought things for the new arrival and showed me how to care for her.

Even though the family tried to be supportive, a crying infant can grate on anyone's nerves; especially in a small 2 bedroom apartment where everyone had to work in the morning. So, as soon as possible, Richard and I moved into our own inexpensive apartment. Caring for a baby was hard. The feedings and diapers, the loads of laundry and sleepless nights began to catch up on me. She was a colicky baby; she would cry for hours. By Christmas I was exhausted. I turned on Richard.

"You never help with this baby. When I was pregnant you promised to help out, you never even change her diaper. All you ever do is go out. When she cries you can't stand it so you run out of here. Do you think I like it? Do you think it's easy for me?" I screamed at him.

"Of course not, I know it's hard, it's hard for me too. I have to work at that boring job and for peanuts. I'm sorry if I don't help with the baby, but I can't stand it when she cries. You are so much better at it than I am," he answered.

"Because I have to be, I have no choice. If I don't take care of her, who will? I'm so bored here. I want to get out more. I thought I would get a job or go back to school after she was born," I said through my tears.

"You can't, the baby needs you. A mother should be with her baby, not be sending her to a babysitter. It's your job." Richard's chauvinist tendencies finally surfaced.

"My job, so what is your job, hanging around with your friends? Enjoying life while I suffer through mine?" I screamed and ran to our bedroom slamming the door behind me. This woke the baby and she started wailing. I tried to ignore it, let him take care of her for once. After ten minutes, the baby was still crying. Richard knocked softly, "I'm going out," he called through the door. I heard the outside door slam.

So I sat alone on New Year's Eve. Richard had gone out with his friends. Other girls my age were out partying or maybe making some spending money babysitting for a neighbor. I was also babysitting, but for myself. No parents would arrive at 1:00 in the morning flushed and a tiny bit drunk, to pay me off for minding their child. I felt like my life was insufferable. How would I go on? I had never been so miserable. What a terrible mistake I'd made.

But I did go on. My daughter, Stephanie, grew up. Richard and I have remained together through some very rough times. I adjusted to being a mother. I accepted that my life would never be the same but that it could still be good. My "baby" is fifteen years old now and is an honor roll student at her high school. She plays classical piano and loves sports. She has shelves full of trophies and academic awards from school. She seems happy and well adjusted and talks of becoming a lawyer when she grows up.

Sometimes I am so afraid for her. I, too, had big plans and big dreams for my future. One decision changed all that. Today, I attend night courses at the University and I work in an office. My job is boring but I still dream of a brighter future; I think I can reach it someday.

I now know that I am proud of the job I did, raising my daughter. When I was seventeen, I didn't realize what an important thing I was doing. I may have had to postpone a few things in my life but I have been so enriched by having a daughter. She has brought so much to my life. I see now just how much I have learned and gained. I have become a much more responsible person and experienced a love and job that many people may never know. My daughter and I grew up together. Today, we share our taste in clothes, music, and movies. Of course, we don't agree on everything and argue constantly, just like sisters do.

I am so proud of Stephanie. Many people, including my daughter's high school principal, have told me that I did a wonderful job raising her; that she is a great kid.

These past years were at times very difficult; at times very wonderful, I wouldn't trade my time with my daughter for anything in the world.

(Written by Mom)

And that was how it all began, our life as a little family. No drum roll, no red carpet, but a whole lot of love and a whole lot of hope. Our little family was spit out into the world to be devoured, challenged, and tested. Mom should have become a doctor or a writer. But instead, she was stuck with a difficult decision of having a baby at age sixteen or not. It was HER decision. Sure, she had the influence of my father, her mother, mother-in-law, and the world around her to become a mother. But, ultimately, the decision was hers. She could have taken her life and this baby's life into her own hands and taken the easy way out. Mom was too honest and too responsible to think of only herself. She had gotten herself into this situation and she was going to hold herself accountable. She would make the most of this situation. She was hopeful life would pay her back some way. Hopeful that everything would work out great. She knew she had enough love to bring a child into the world.

At that point, I became her life. I was her only purpose and she would never let me down. She was going to spend every waking hour teaching me and inspiring me. She lived to help me become the best at anything I wanted to do and fill my mind with aspirations and dreams. She shared the world's possibilities and dangers with me. I was not only her life, I was life itself. I lived the life she had always wanted for herself. She would not allow me to be faced with the very difficult decisions she had been faced with. She also encouraged me to try everything, living vicariously through me. I was able to do all the things she had not, yet, had the chance to do.

FAMILY

I am who I am today because of how my parents raised me and what my family has inspired me to become. My family of two great parents, two grandmothers, uncles, aunts and cousins has surrounded me since birth. Each has a special personality which has taught me right from wrong and whom I wanted to be like. I have shared every moment of my life with my family and feel a strong alliance with them. I have so many memories of times spent together, both good and bad, and I cherish every one of those memories.

Mom and Dad were young when they had me and all of Dad's siblings had their children young too. The brothers and sisters were together almost daily so the children could play together. My cousins were my first friends and have remained my best friends throughout my entire life. I have never gone more than a few days without speaking with my cousins. We were all in this together and all helped when we could. I would sleep over regularly at Aunt Darlene's house because Cousin Kathy was my best friend. Mom and Dad didn't have to worry about me spending the night at a stranger's house. I would ask Mom if I could spend the night at Kathy's and she would drop me off. Oddly enough though, I would not be able to sleep; I would toss and turn until finally, I would get out of bed and walk over to Aunt Darlene's room crying. I missed my mother and wanted to call her to come pick me up. I couldn't spend a night away from my mother. I missed her too much if I didn't see her for a few hours. I would call Mom at two in the morning every time I tried to sleep over and she would drive right over to pick me up. I think she was happy when I called her because she probably missed me too. She never once said "No, I'll come first thing in the morning." Instead she always replied quickly "I'll be right over honey, give me ten minutes. You can take a nap on the couch at Auntie's house and I'll carry you out when I get there." I did this repeatedly and she never once complained about this common routine.

Sure enough, I would wake up in the morning in my own bed. Poor cousin Kathy would call me in the morning, "What happened? Where did you go?"

And I would reply "I missed my mother!"

She never teased me. Everyone knew I was mommy's girl. They all said I was "spoiled" but never teased me.

Mami, Papi Castagnier and Nanny Sugrue were a huge part of my life. They babysat me from birth; while Mom and Dad worked. I loved spending time with them because I could pretty much do whatever I wanted. I could empty the entire pantry to play store with Kathy and no one ever said a word. There was always some cousin over at Mami and Papi's being babysat to play with. Kathy would come over all the time. Dad's sister Darlene had two children, Kathy and Marco. Kathy is a year and a half younger than me and Marco is two months younger. They were the closest to me in age so we always played together. They lived on the first level of Mami and Papi's duplex in Ville St-Pierre. Their other son, Jacky and aunt Christiane lived upstairs with their two daughters Melanie and Melissa. Melanie is almost three years older than me and Melissa is two years younger than I am. It is easy to understand why I loved spending time with my cousins. They were always around and we were all the same age. Our parents were all brothers and sisters and forced us to get along and support each other. We would play together for hours. Our parents taught us the value of family. We supported each cousin's activities. When one of us sang at a choir performance for Christmas, the entire family showed up. We were at every event together and spent every holiday together.

Dad's younger brother, Uncle Gary and Aunt Josee didn't have kids yet but lived together. Uncle Gary was my Godfather and took his job as Godfather very seriously. He looked after me the most and I always felt special to him. He played the drums, which I always admired, seeing as no one else in the family played a musical instrument. With my passion for piano, I felt we had the most in common. Uncle Gary was so much like my father too; which I loved. He was personable and passionate about our family and about life. He wanted all of us to achieve any dream we had and would help whenever he could. Uncle Gary was the type of man that would literally give you the shirt off his back if you were cold. He was the life of the family and always planned our family parties and dinners. Uncle Gary kept our family together for years and you could just feel his love radiate through his shining blue eyes. Uncle Gary had so many qualities; the family values Papi Castagnier had, the passion my Dad had, the sincerity my Mother had, and the intelligence to do the right thing or at least to try to. Uncle Gary has always been there for me and his presence has been a driving force in my life.

I have many childhood memories with my family. We all gathered for the summer weekends and vacations at our family Chalet at Lac St-Paul. The same should be said for Halloween, Birthdays, Christmas, New Years; basically every weekend and holidays were spent with the family. There was always some birthday party or family BBQ being planned. We had a big extended family and were all very much a part of each other's lives. All our friends were envious of our family because we were all so close. It is rare to see families so close in this day and age. We were all proud to be a part of each other's lives and to be so close. We were one big happy family!!

On Mom's side was Nanny, Uncle Peter and Aunt Sachiko. Mom's sister, Aunt Maureen her husband, Doug, and daughter, Heather.

Dad was the life of the family. He was making loads of money so he often bought his brothers and sister gifts for no specific reason. He was Melanie's Godfather and bought her a mini motor cycle for her eighth birthday. Dad threw a major Christmas party one year, renting a hall and a DJ. The entire family came, the Castagniers and Mami's family from Lachute. There must have been over one hundred-fifty of us and Dad had Santa give gifts to EVERYONE!

Everyone loved Dad and Dad loved how giving made him feel. I was so proud to have a father who was so charismatic and loving. He would carry me on his shoulders everywhere we went. I was definitely "daddy's little girl" then. He did the fun stuff and Mom took care of me. I was really spoiled by my parents. I got any toy I wanted and had new jewelry all the time. I even got one of those mini motor cycles too, at the same time Melanie got hers. When Dad asked me what I wanted for my sixth birthday I said, "a red Corvette". Sure enough, on my sixth birthday, a real red Corvette was sitting outside our apartment. He said he would drive it until I was old enough to have it. Mom was outraged about the gift saying he had really exaggerated this time.

I loved riding my motorcycle. Dad taught me to ride a motorcycle before I learned how to ride a bicycle! Dad would ride his Harley and I would ride my Suzuki 50 along side him. We would drive all around town. I was six years old and was driving down the highway on my motorcycle with Dad on his Harley beside me riding to the ice cream parlor. Dad loved it. He loved how courageous I was and always up for anything. I was never afraid and tried everything. I was a little tomboy and would wear my little leather jacket, jeans, and biker boots to go riding. He was so proud of me all the time. Cars passing by would honk at us cheering us on and Dad loved the attention I got. He said I could do anything I wanted. He told everyone that one day his daughter was going to become the Prime Minister of Canada or the President of Nike. He would say, "My daughter is going to be the one in charge." He taught me to be confident in myself and that I could do anything. He taught me to try anything because I would not know if I could do it unless I at least tried.

I watched him lead his friends and family. He was always the leader and always telling people what the plan for the day was. He was in charge and everyone was happy to follow him. Everyone loved and admired him. He also had a great sense of vision and always thought big. His thoughts were always on how to make some business venture nationwide or how to expand businesses to the next level. He always thought about the big picture. He always was full of new ideas on business opportunities and family activities. He was on top of the world and the family was always around us.

He would buy truck loads of fireworks and set them off at our family chalet. We had continuous parties at the chalet and Dad bought all the food and alcohol. He even bought me a school bus to play in at the chalet as my clubhouse. Kathy and I ran the school house and told everyone they needed a password to get on. The password never existed so Kathy and I played on the bus alone for hours.

Dad bought speed boats, water skis, four wheelers, dirt bikes, and bicycles for the chalet. Everyone was welcome to use any of the toys whenever they wanted. These were family toys; for everyone. He bought all these things for the family and never thought of any of it as "his" stuff. He always said it was the "family's" stuff.

Even though Dad was always up for a party and having everyone around, my fondest memories at the chalet with the family was when Dad and I were alone. We would get up in the morning and Dad would always pull me aside at the breakfast table and ask, "Want to go for a boat ride just the two of us?" I would jump in his arms and we would run to the dock after breakfast. I looked forward to his invitation in the morning and almost expected our boat rides alone when we were up there. No one else could come, it was our time. We would take a canoe and ride off for hours, looking for secret passages and other parts of the big lake we had not seen. We would take turns ramming the oars and getting the boat to move as quickly as we could. We discovered a secret tunnel with lilly pads and frogs hopping around. It was beautiful and peaceful. We talked about life and about everything that was going on those days. He would ask me what I wanted to become when I was older and what my dreams were. He would tell me how much he loved Mom and what a wonderful person she was. He would talk about how strong she was and how lucky he was to have us both. He would tell me how happy he was and that this was his favorite place in the world. He shared his dreams for me and constantly gave me ideas on what to become later in life and where to visit. He filled my mind and imagination with all sorts of exciting thoughts and dreams. He told me I should become a high powered lawyer or a wealthy stock broker. He said the most important thing was for me to be as educated as I could and to arm myself with all the tools I needed. He told me to listen first to everything being said around me, then force my way to the top. He said the one on top was always the one who believed they deserved to be there. He said I should always think I deserved to be the best because I would work the hardest to get there.

One time, we took one of the speed boats for a ride. We went so far and were so wrapped up in our conversation that we ran out of gas. Dad rammed us to the closest shore in hopes of finding someone who could drive us back to our chalet. We couldn't find anyone so started walking back. Neither of us had shoes on because we were not expecting to walk. He carried me on his shoulders for two hours as we walked back to our chalet; both in our bathing suites under the scorching sun. We were still very far from the chalet when our Aunt Murielle, thankfully, drove past us on her way into town to run errands. She recognized us and quickly turned around. She asked us what the hell we were doing walking down the highway in our bathing suits! We explained our adventure as she drove us the rest of the way back. Dad's feet were severely blistered from walking on the burning pavement. I felt so bad; I brought a bucket filled with cold water over to him on the couch to soak his feet. Dad looked up at me with the biggest smile saying "Honey, I would walk on fire any day for you, you are my life and I would do anything. Always remember that sweetie, you are everything to me and today was the best day of my life" as he pulled me over for a hug. I melted in his arms and Mom put both her arms around us both.

Dad was great. He was loving, successful, charismatic, flooded us with affection, loved Mom, and adored me. This was the happiest we could ever be.

We had our family chalet for many years but after Papi died, Mami said she was tired of doing all the work so she sold it without telling any of us. After Papi died, everything changed. The chalet was gone, Mami and the whole family were depressed, and things at home slowly began to change.

WHAT GOES UP

The many enjoyable memories from my childhood are pleasant and happy. I had a good life early on. We had lots of money; the family was healthy and happy. Mom and Dad were in love and had talked about giving me a brother or sister. I was the best student at school and Mom and Dad showered me with love and affection. I was on top of the world right along side my mother and father. But, unfortunately, in life you tend to remember the really bad times more than the good. I was younger when our life together was simple and happy. The good memories fade as I grew older. Unfortunately, the bad memories are the most vivid now.

I was twelve or thirteen years old when the tide started to turn. Mom worked as a clerk for a courier company and Dad was starting to change. Dad was furious at first when Mom got that job. He had a conservative mentality, where the man worked and the woman stayed home. He thought a real man should make enough money for the whole family. Eventually, he caved in and allowed her to work. The money was a nice compliment and Mom felt independent. Mom was allowed to work but not allowed to make any friends; especially male friends. Dad was a very jealous man. He always accused Mom of trying to attract men's attention if she looked "too good" before heading out. The accusations made her uncertain about her appearance so she tried to tone down her natural beauty as best she could. She wore no make up, her hair was flat and plain, and she wore loose fitting, unflattering, clothes. It almost looked as though her plan, in the morning, was to look as bad as she possibly could. She felt guilty if she tried to make herself look pretty. I always encouraged her to wear lip stick or to try tying her hair back in different ways. But she refused and said that I could experiment on her at night when we were home alone. She said she preferred to be plain and not get any bad attention. She said she didn't want any problems. She respected Dad's wishes and just wanted to play it safe.

The once courageous and playful girl she was in her youth became a timid and shy adult with my father. I think Dad just took up so much space in the world that there was no space for her. She happily took a back seat behind my father since he said and did things she could never even imagine saying to anyone. Dad was not afraid of anything and Mom became afraid of everything.

Mom would speak to others with her head down and always with some uncertainty. She had a sweet and charming air about her which enchanted most. She was intriguing and the words she chose to speak were always intelligent and meaningful.

Around the time Mom started to work, Dad began to be challenged by his demons. Being the big time drug dealer that he was, he had unlimited access to massive quantities of drugs. He had always enjoyed a frequent joint but after Papi died, he quickly moved on to acid and experimenting with other drugs. Once the drug he used had little to no effect, he graduated to the next level. Eventually, he was consuming more than he was selling. He moved into heavy doses of coke. It was a rapid free-fall from coke to shooting up crack. He would justify this new habit to us and the world as "a required escape from the frequent nightmares of loosing his father."

He was living the life of a true rock star. Money, parties, women, and drugs. Lots of it all. His business had grown to a separate apartment in Montreal, an apartment in New York, suppliers in Mexico, boats and planes to transport it all to Miami, and then into Canada. Dad had moved into the major league. He supposedly was even on the "U.S. Most Wanted Drug Dealer" list with the large operation he had in the States. All his bases were covered. He grew it in Mexico, boats brought it into Miami, planes brought it to New York, and trucks drove it up into Canada. He had built one of the biggest drug dealing operation in Canada and the U.S.

Throughout this rise to his throne, Mom and I lived our simple life in our little downtown city apartment. We saw Dad less and less. He came home when he felt like it, barging in unannounced. He lived the life of a bachelor with the security of a wife and child at home. He enjoyed the best of both worlds. He was addicted to the power. Mom tried to talk to him to see what he was doing all the time because she thought maybe he might be losing control. He always assured her, "It's only for another year, then I'm done, be patient."

ROCK STAR STUMBLES BACK HOME

One day, Dad came home for good. He said he needed help. He had lost control. He said he was high all the time and everyone was stealing from him. He said he closed down most of his operation because he couldn't trust anyone anymore. He said he would wake up in the morning and not remember what city he was in. It was all so sudden but we were glad to just have him back. We didn't know half of what he had been living and didn't want to know.

Dad was able to support his drug addiction for about a year with the reserves of money he had stashed away. He was so caught up in his drugs, falling deeper and deeper into its grasp, that he was falling into an abyss of no return. Soon, there was absolutely no money coming in but Mom's little clerical salary. Thank God she had insisted on taking that job because, now, it was the only thing keeping the three of us alive.

Dad sold off all his toys. The cars, motorcycles, and four-wheelers were all sniffed and shot up. Then the jewelry, remaining bags of money in the basement, and little money Mom had managed to save up in their bank accounts were injected into his forearms. Then, total desperation. Dad had sold and consumed everything he and Mom had ever worked for and had earned in their lives. It was all gone. So how was he going to shoot up tonight, became his only concern.

He began with petty robberies. He robbed clothing stores, jewelry stores, and even houses. He often got caught because he was high and stumbled out of the scene of the crime. He was in and out of jail, one week here, two months there. If we ever wondered where Dad was, he was either shooting up in the park, sleeping in his bed, or in jail.

Eventually, robbing strangers was too much work. He resorted to robbing us. He sold our jewelry one night. Our electronics another night. Our fancy clothes and our nice furniture. Anything nice we ever had was all taken back. He wasn't selling our stuff fast enough to support his need. He came home one morning and said "Nancy, I have hit rock bottom. I can't do this anymore. I need help. Find me a rehab place and take me there right away."

Mom and I were relieved. We couldn't take it anymore either and still had a shred of dignity left to pull our family back together. We were extremely supportive. We felt sorry for him and wanted to help the great man we still loved.

His first rehab was up in the North suburbs somewhere called DoReMi. We didn't have a car anymore so Mami drove us all up there to drop Dad off. It was a three week program which followed a strict boot camp type of regime. He had to scrub floors and attend classes. He hated it. He hated to have to swallow his pride and be someone's slave. He had been the boss man and to be downgraded to scrubbing floors was his hell.

It was winter and freezing as usual in Quebec. Mom and I could only visit him on weekends due to the program's strict rules. So all three weekends we would pack a big bag of goodies and letters we wrote him during the week; telling him how proud we were and how much we loved him. He needed us now and we were there to help him through. Years before, he had loved us unconditionally so now, it was our turn to step up and love him unconditionally. We didn't care about all the material stuff we had lost. We still had each other and would rebuild when he was better.

Mom and I would sit together in the kitchen and read our letters out loud. We were happy to be pulling together. Dad began to say to both of us, while he was at that rehab, the words always on his mind were "united we stand, divided we fall." He said he was going to change and that we were going to be the family we once were long ago. He said together we would get through this.

Mom and I used the public transportation system to get all the way up north on the weekends to visit. We had to change bus routes twice and travel over two hours to DoReMi. That last weekend, we walked back to the bus stop late Sunday night. Mom and I both stood under the bus sign, anticipating the two little yellow bus lights to appear over the white snowy horizon. It was the coldest night I have ever remembered in my life. The snow had begun to fall heavily and quickly turned into the worst snow blizzard of the season. The heavy wet snow was sinking through our jackets and we were now wet and freezing. Our teeth chattered loudly and jaws clenched tightly to our freezing teeth. I remember thinking to myself that my ears would fall off if we had to wait another twenty minutes for the bus to arrive. Late in the evening, buses that far north of the city only ran every thirty minutes and we had just missed the last bus as we walked up to the sign. Mom and I were so tightly bundled up that we could only see each other's eye lashes. Mom caught frost bite on her cheeks that night because her scarf was not thick enough.

Dad was just so happy to see us visit him that the pain of getting there was all worth it. When he saw us walk through the front entrance to the rehab building he would literally run over to us like a boy running to his father at an airport. It was the best feeling in the world; knowing we were helping him and all this attention was working. He was positive and his counselors said he had made tremendous progress. He learned all these new prayers and had a restored faith in life and in God.

He came out of that first rehab a changed man. He was full of life and started working out again. He started thinking about new "legal" business opportunities. He had tons of ideas as usual, all which made complete sense. Dad could never work for anyone else. He said most people were incompetent and he could never work for anyone incompetent. And besides, he said he could do the job better than anyone else. He was right. I never met anyone as capable and business savvy as my father. I could never imagine him working for someone else. He would drive his boss crazy and run him out of his own business to take it over himself. Dad started a rose business with Mom, where he had women selling roses in fancy restaurants for five dollars a rose. He actually made hundreds of dollars a night with these pretty women selling roses. All three of us would wrap the roses in clear paper on Wednesday night for the weekend. He was back on track.

A couple of months later, he said unannounced, "Nancy, I'm going for a walk." We didn't think much of his abrupt announcement because we naively thought he had really changed. We didn't see him for a week. He came back looking like he had been back to hell. The first time he fell back after rehab was the biggest let down. After all the effort and hard work all three of us had made, we went back to where we started. I felt betrayed and confused. Where had we gone wrong? Did I do enough to help? Dad picked right back up where he had left off.

He would sleep a few days; wake up and cry a few hours asking us to forgive him. Then, we all hugged and thought it was finally over. Later, he would go for a walk, come back after few days, cry with us for a few hours and we all hugged. This went on and on, over and over. It was like an old record player, where the record would skip at the same place over and over again. He just couldn't break the pattern of getting up then crashing back down.

He was in and out of every rehab in town. Sometimes, he made it through the entire program but, most times, he quit and would call us to come pick him up with his mother's car. Mom and I followed him around like little puppies, always hopeful this was it. I guess we had no choice but to be hopeful and keep trying. What were our alternatives? I loved my father and he needed me. I couldn't abandon him when he needed me. I am sure Mom felt the same. She did everything she possibly could think of to try to help him. She never yelled at him, never judged him, and never degraded him. She encouraged him and sympathized with him. I have never known anyone to give themselves as completely as she did. She truly and unconditionally loved this man and was going to do whatever she had to do to help him get out of his hell.

WHAT COMES AFTER ROCK BOTTOM?

Slowly, Mom and I grew tired of the rollercoaster we had been riding on for almost two years. We eventually came to the realization that no matter how much we tried to change him, he was the only one who could change himself. Dad went to Narcotics Anonymous meetings while Mom and I went to Alanon meetings, which were for the families of addicts. Since the rehabs didn't work maybe daily meetings would? Dad went to every meeting he could possibly fit in a day.

He constantly promised, "Nancy, this is it, I have hit rock bottom this time and can't go on. I am changing my life today." He must have claimed to hit rock bottom twenty times that same year. It was that old broken record again, repeating the same line over and over. We began to think maybe he didn't just hit rock bottom but actually fell right down through the floor.

Nothing changed. Actually, things got worst. He just kept getting worst. Just when we thought things couldn't get any worst, he hit a new low. By this time, I was fourteen years old, soon to be fifteen. Mami and the rest of the family had slowly been pushed out or just basically crept out of our lives. I figured that they all had their own lives to worry about and just didn't know how to deal with my father or us. It always was disturbing to wonder where everyone had gone. No one bothered to call us or wondered where we were? Didn't they worry about if we were still alive? We didn't hear from the family for months at a time.

I was severely depressed, humiliated, and fearful for our lives now. Dad fell deeper and deeper into heavy, dangerous doses of drugs. He was gone during the day and returned during the night to rampage and loot our house. He was so high that he was not coherent enough to rob anymore. He brought home strange men with him who also took things from our house to settle their recent sale of drugs to Dad. I was afraid for Mom and me that these strange men who would stroll through the house during the night with my zombie father would rape us; so, I slept with mom in her bed now. I had moved from sleeping in my own bed to sleeping on the floor behind my door. If my door was opened, it would hit me and I would have time to wake up. I would be able to run to my window and jump out into the alley behind the house. I had a whole emergency exit planned out in my mind and would go over my security exit before falling asleep. But, after a few nights of assuring myself I had found a safe way out, I would worry about how Mom would make it out. So I decided to get up from sleeping on the floor to being brave and sleeping with Mom in her bed with her. At least the two of us together might have a chance at fighting them off. We slept with a baseball bat under our bed and I kept a kitchen knife under my side of the mattress. I slept with Mom every night from that point on. We held hands through the night and our dog Corey slept at our feet. This bed was our life raft that we were safe in together. I fell asleep imagining that our mattress had an imaginary force field around it and no one could break in. I probably would have stabbed anyone who came close to our bed while we lay there. Neither of us got much sleep ever at all. The door would fling open every couple of hours; the noise or the cold from outside would constantly wake us.

PRISONERS

I never brought friends or boyfriends home. I was embarrassed of how poor we were and how bare our house was. I began to frequently lash out at myself in anger. That's when the cutting began. I started with minor cuts on my stomach while I showered then, eventually, moved into locking myself in the bathroom for an hour, trying to cut myself as painfully as I could. I would cut myself in hidden places on my stomach and thighs with a small blade so as not to alarm the outside world. It was my way of letting out the pain that I felt inside. Even today, it is difficult for me to explain how this could possibly have made me feel better. It just felt good knowing I felt the pain in one particular place rather than hurting all over inside.

Life had to go on for Mom and I during the day. We led two different lives. During the day, I was an honor roll student, captain of the volleyball team, best friend to a few, first sweetheart to a few, and most likely to succeed by my peers and teachers. For all they knew, I was from a wealthy white collar family living in a fancy home in the burbs. I did not look like I woke up every morning from our night through hell with my blond hair and clean polished look.

Mom continued to work at her courier job as a clerk and was in charge of writing instruction manuals for the company in addition to her daily duties. Her boss praised her work quality and endless potential. She was seen as a rising star to the management staff and someone they were keeping an eye on for the next promotion.

Mom worked in a retail office in old Montreal. I would finish school and take the bus to her office so we could ride back home together. It was out of my way but I looked forward to spending time with her; a couple more hours, just the two of us, before heading back to reality. She worked alone all day, in that small office, so she looked forward to my company at the end of her long work day. We would share stories about our days. She would tell me about all the interesting people she had met that day and where they were from. Since she worked for a shipping company, she conversed with clients all over the world. She would fantasize about places she wanted us to visit some day together.

It was November and most of the company's full time employees were on strike. Mom had been hired as a temporary employee so she had to continue

47

to work as she was not part of the union. One day, we were sitting in the office having our usual afternoon conversation when several hysterical strikers stormed in. They tore through the office and threw all the paper trays upside down and were screaming viciously at Mom "You scab, you whore, what are you doing stealing our jobs!" One of the angry women pushed my mother roughly aside to get behind the counter. There was such intense fear in my mother's eyes as she hit the wall behind her with a loud thump. She shuddered quietly and was obviously hurt. I was so enraged that I ran up behind this woman and tackled her as hard as I could from behind. She fell to the ground roughly and I knelt down on top of her with my knee pressed down hard on her upper back. I screamed out loud, "Everybody, get the hell out of here now or I'll call the police and seriously hurt your fat friend under here."

The women were all in shock, Mom included. Everyone just stood there looking down at me. The four other women walked out quickly and I let the woman up from under my knee and told her, "None of you better even think about coming back here because the police will be here waiting."

No one ever came back from the striker squad. Mom's first words were, "Damn, those sports sure are paying off! You had me convinced. Good thing I didn't sign you up for Karate." We both giggled and hugged. We looked into each other's eyes knowing we always had each other to count on. If one of us was hurt, the other was always there to help. It was us against the world. Mom and I were best friends and fought the world every day and every night together. The last thing we needed was some stupid strikers pushing us around. We had our fair share of being pushed around by Dad and it wasn't going to happen again by some stranger if I could help it.

We would ride home together on the bus in the early evening, never knowing what awaited us at home. I never wanted to go straight home from school in fear of what I would find. Sometimes, there were strangers in the house shooting up in the living room with no sign of Dad. Other times, Dad was partying in the hot tub in the basement with two naked hookers. These strangers would go through our clothes and felt free to make themselves at home. The most common scenario was when Dad was passed out on the bathroom floor with a needle still sticking in his arm.

I always had a sick uneasy feeling in the pit of my stomach as we unlocked the front door. I held my breath and hoped today wouldn't be too bad. I was always more concerned about the pain and humiliation it caused my mother than fear for myself. I would try to make her feel better;

"I'll get them out Mom." "Don't worry Mom, they're leaving now." "I'll pick him up off the floor with you Ma." "It's OK Mum. Don't cry. It'll get better soon." "No need yelling at them all, they're all stoned and can't hear you anyways, let's just get them out of here." Mom and I cleaned the mess every day when we came home. There were lines of coke on the coffee table and used dirty needles scattered all around the house. The house was filthy and all our spoons were burnt and bent. The spoons were used to melt the crack into a liquid to shoot up. The floors were muddy and the carpets were soiled. The beds were used and the sheets were on the floor. Every day, a piece of my insides was ripped out. The devil had possessed my helpless father and was not showing any mercy. He was brining hell right back to our home and shoving it right in our faces.

Mom and I slowly lost hope and any dream we had of Dad fighting these demons. I started wishing and praying at night to God to do something, anything. I prayed that God might help Dad beat this. Then, after a while, I prayed that he would take Dad away, send him to jail for a while to clean him up. Then, I prayed that he just burn the house down so we could move somewhere better. Maybe a fresh new start could help Dad? In the end, I just prayed to God to just take me away. I prayed that I would just stop breathing and die quietly in the night. I prayed to get hit by a bus or have a heart attack while out jogging.

I slowly became mad at Mom for not getting us out of there. It was dangerous for us there. No one was around to save us and we didn't know how or where to get help. Dad threatened us not to tell anyone about the life we lived. He would tell us, "No one gives a f*** about us in this family anymore. The good times are over and they have all abandoned us, it is just the three us of now." He was right; it was just the three of us left in the world. He was humiliated and too proud to let anyone else know how bad we were struggling.

We were alienated from the world. Eventually, I began to convince Mom that we had to get out of there or he would kill us. We started looking for an apartment we could afford in Rosemont, near my high school. I was fifteen years old and remember this day well. Dad came home stoned that morning and Mom was upset as usual.

She lashed back at him, "We're moving Richard. We started looking for an apartment and were leaving as soon as I can find somewhere for us to live."

Dad said nothing. He just pulled the covers up over his dirty body and fell asleep. I thought to myself as I got dressed for school that his response was odd. He must not care anymore? We hadn't had a real conversation with him for almost two years. Maybe he had lost his mind? All the drugs had fried the few remaining brain cells he had left?

The next night, he left as usual. He came back around 1:00 AM for round one of the looting.

As he slammed open the door, he yelled out as loud as he could, "Nancy, I am warning you now. Can you hear me, damn it?"

"Yes, I'm up, what is it?" she moaned softly.

He slowly articulated with an eerie tone, "If you f***in leave here with my daughter, I will find you. And when I find you, I will kill you both!"

He had an empty stare as he held her by the neck against the wall in the hallway. He held her there for what felt like five minutes, as if waiting for the words to really sink in. She said nothing. Tears flowed endlessly down her check as she stared down at her bare feet. I thought she might not be touching the floor as he was strangling her. I heard the beginning of the conversation from my bed but was now standing a few feet away looking up at them.

I yelled, "Dad, stop it. You're hurting her. She can't breath!" and tears ran down my face.

He didn't look at me and let go of Mom. He had been holding her neck so tightly that his hand was imprinted on her skin. She said nothing. We both stood barefoot in the hall as Dad brushed past me to go into my room. He took my gym shoes that I had hidden with me under my covers while I slept.

I yelled, "No Dad, please don't take my shoes, I have a basketball game tomorrow. I need those to play. Here, take my coat instead," and I handed him my winter coat.

He grabbed my winter coat and walked past me with the coat and shoes still in his hands. Mom and I didn't look at each other. We didn't say a word, we just stood silently against the wall as we watched Dad walk out into the cold night. We slowly walked back into her room and turned off all the lights. We lay in bed silently without emotion, her cold hand in mine. I had cried so much these last few years that there were no tears left to hold back. I was numb.

We both knew moving out into an apartment was too dangerous. He meant every word he said, he would find us and he would kill us. He had nothing else to live for now and if we left he would have nothing to lose. We stopped looking for apartments but Mom made some calls to some abuse shelters. Mom did not want us to leave our house to live in a shelter; she was afraid of the effect it would have on me.

We talked about it and realized that the effects of staying in the abusive environment were worse than the effects of living in a shelter. We visited some shelters but they were all just "temporary" shelters; where you could only stay for a few nights. We needed something more stable, more long-term. There was one shelter for abused women in Vancouver where they made you change your identity; for safety purposes. We are so desperate that we thought we should give it a try. Maybe he would forget about us if we were far away and he would not come looking for us. After a few months or a year, we could move back to Montreal and start over, just the two of us. We added our names to their program and they said there was a three year waiting list! We kept looking for other options, keeping the Vancouver possibility in the back of our minds. Hopefully, something would open up and we wouldn't have to wait three more years. I prayed everyday that they would call us with good news, that it was our turn to go.

EMPTY

We had nothing left. Nothing left in the house, no more money in the bank accounts, we had no food in the fridge, no clothes in our dressers, no couch in the living room, no T.V. to watch, and no dignity left in us. Mom and I said nothing to each other in the morning. We got dressed and had no food left to pack our lunches. I had no lunch money either but lied and told Mom I had five dollars hidden in my locker at school. I didn't care to eat anymore; I'd rather just skip lunch. I didn't care much about anything. I called my friend Jack, who lived down the street, after my Dad took my shoes and winter coat and asked, "Jack, sorry to bother you but would you mind lending me your gym shoes for the day?" I didn't say why and he never asked. He quickly replied "Of course, I'll be at your house in five minutes".

I walked over to Mom before we both headed out for the day and we quietly hugged. We never spoke of that night again; we both let go of the dream of moving out on our own. We did not speak of moving again. Our routine continued as it was for a few more months.

My cutting was worse than ever at this point. I had over twenty cuts on my stomach and thighs at all times. Mom walked in on me one day as I got out of the shower. She looked at me in pure shock and panic.

"What have you done to yourself Steph?" she cried. "I'm ok Mom, just please get out." She waited for me by the bathroom door to come out. "We need to talk about this," she pleaded.

"Mom, I'm fine. It just makes me feel better. It's harmless. And besides, I have been doing this for a couple of years and I'm fine."

"Well, I don't want you doing it anymore, please promise you won't do this again?" tears built up in her eyes and trickled down her pale cheeks.

"OK, Mom I won't anymore, I promise."

The last thing I wanted to do was cause her any more pain that she already was forced to endure. So I made sure my door was locked when I took my shower and continued privately.

Mom became frequently sick. She had constant colds, infections, even pneumonias. Doctors couldn't explain what was wrong with her. My sixteenth birthday was coming up and Mom had managed to save up and hide a little money. She had talked to my best friend Sandra's parents one day about surprising me for my sweet sixteen. She wanted to surprise me with an airplane ticket to Portugal for the summer with Sandra and her family. I had talked about Sandra's family vacations back to Portugal for years. They invited me to go with them every year but I didn't even ask Mom. I knew there was no way we could ever afford it. Most importantly, there was no way I was ever going to leave my mother alone. I had never spent one night away from her and had grown accustomed to sleeping with her now.

On the day of my sixteenth birthday, Mom gave me her gift with huge excitement and joy—an airplane ticket to Portugal. She had paid for this ticket with money she had saved secretly for two years. She wanted me to spend the summer away from hell in a beautiful country, on the ocean with Sandra's loving family. I should have known something was up. She didn't trust anyone with me and didn't want to spend any time apart either. For her to send me off for the summer, something had to definitely be wrong.

At first I didn't want to go. "Thank you so much Mom. This is the most incredible gift in the world. I can't believe it," as I hugged her and cried.

"But I can't go now. I don't want to leave you alone. Your cold is really bad this time and I want to stay here and take care of you."

"No, no," she smiled "I want you to go. It was my dream to give you this gift for your sixteenth birthday. I just have a little cold for God's sake. I'll be fine! I want you to go for both of us. We'll write every day and I'll see it all through your eyes!" She was so happy and excited. I had to go and live this to make her happy. So I planned on going on one condition, that we would write each other every day.

I left a couple of weeks later. I was nervous about leaving her. I had an uneasy queasy feeling in my stomach. With Dad in jail for a month again, it shouldn't be too bad for Mom. I would hear from her every day so, if I felt she needed me, I would just come back early. At least, that is how I justified leaving to myself.

I went to Portugal and loved it. It was beautiful and everything I had imagined. I spent my days swimming at the beach and lounging in the cafes with Sandra. We walked around the cobble stoned streets and visited the beautiful churches. My time away from home was like a dream. I floated on air and felt like a princess in a far away land. I knew I had to soak it all in to give Mom as much details as possible. The people walking the streets and sleeping in hammocks at the beach were happy and relaxed. I had never seen this sort of life before. They worked a little in the morning, then napped after lunch for "siesta", and worked a few more hours in the afternoon before heading home to their families. It was a slower pace than I had ever been used to and people there just seemed to exhale a few more seconds with each breath. I loved the pace and thought I could get used to this and live here forever. The food was great and the people interesting.

Although I enjoyed my vacation enormously, I never really did get let go and enjoy it because in the back of my mind, I worried constantly about my mother. I worried about her safety and about her facing those demons alone. I felt guilty for not being there to help and guilty about the danger I left her in. I had a hard time sleeping in Portugal because I worried about Mom up at night, lying in her bed alone, wondering where I was. Although I enjoyed Portugal, I just wanted to come back home. I just could not enjoy it knowing Mom was missing it all. I would rather get home and come back with Mom when we both could experience this in a few years.

I wrote Mom every detail of every day. She wrote a few letters back and then nothing. We had been traveling back and forth from the city house to the mountain house. I figured I probably just missed the mail when we left for the week so tried to convince myself it was nothing. By that point, we had been overseas for four weeks. There were two weeks left. I called home every night and there was no answer. I was definitely panicking. I finally got a hold of Mami and frantically asked, "Is everything ok? I have been writing and calling and Mom has not answered. Is she ok? Where is she?" Mami responded, "She's fine. She had a little pneumonia and is in the hospital. She told me to tell you she is fine and will be back home next week. She said enjoy the rest of your trip and she'll see you when you get home."

"My God Mami, she's in the hospital! I'm coming home right now. I can't believe this, why didn't anyone call me? You all have my number here. I have been going crazy!" I cried.

"She didn't want me to call you. She made me promise not to call you. She said you were making her dream come true by finally visiting Europe and wants you to finish your trip." She explained.

"Where's Dad?" I asked "He is back in again," she answered quickly.

"OK, I am going to talk to Sandra's father and see what I can do, I'll talk to you later," and I hung up as I heard her respond in the background.

I hung the phone up with my heart beating a mile a minute. I ran to Sandra's father and explained that my Mom was in the hospital and I needed to get back right away. He called the airlines but the soonest I could get out was in 5 days. We were leaving in only 10 days so I convinced myself she wanted me to stay here so it couldn't be too serious.

Mom had given me four hundred dollars for spending money for my trip and I had only spent fifty. I was intending to use the money to buy Mom this beautiful diamond ring and a charm bracelet I had spotted on my first visit into town. As we prepared to return back to Canada, I went and bought Mom that ring and bracelet. I was so excited to give them to her. She would be so happy that I brought her back something beautiful instead of spending that money on something useless.

At this point, I desperately wanted to get home. I knew she needed me and I needed her. I cried the entire plane ride back because I felt something just wasn't right. Nothing made sense. Why did she stop writing back? Three letters in over a month? Only three letters? She loved to write. Why didn't she call at least? I had not heard from her in over a month. It just didn't make any sense?

We arrived at Mirabel airport and much to my surprise, the entire Castagnier family was waiting for me at the terminal. My initial response was surprise and happiness. Then, panic quickly set in. Why was everyone here? OK, now I knew something had to be terribly wrong. I kissed everyone and thanked them for coming. Uncle Gary said I was to ride with him. We walked to his car and neither of us said a word. They all saw panic in my face. We sat in Uncle Gary's car and started driving.

"Steph, your mother is in the hospital. She is very sick," he said softly. "Yes, I know, Mami told me. Pneumonia she said?" I asked. "It must be another bad one if she is still in the hospital, when is she being released?" I asked. "Well, they don't know when she is being released. She has some type of virus and they are still running tests," he explained. "Let's go straight to the hospital to see her OK?" I asked. "OK," he replied.

GONE

Neither of us spoke the rest of the way. A virus? I went over the possibilities in my head. That can't be too major. The common cold is a virus so it must be similar. It must be from working in that damp office of hers combined with all the stress and fatigue she had endured that caused this bad virus.

Uncle Gary and I arrived at the Hotel Dieu hospital, which was one street over from our house. It was 10 PM so there was just one nurse on duty with most of the lights dimly lit.

Uncle Gary said, "Hi," to the nurse and said, "This is her," as he pointed at me.

Her, I thought? They had talked about me? How odd. We were on the 7th floor of the hospital and Uncle Gary lead the way down the hall. He walked through the last door and I followed behind him.

I looked around the room and didn't see my mother. He walked over to the bed to a figure I had never seen. I thought we must be in the wrong room. This shape hidden under the covers was tiny and looked like a child.

"She's sleeping," he whispered. "That can't be mo—oom ..." as I inched to take a closer look in disbelief. My body was trembling and my knees were about to give out. I was suddenly nauseous and forced myself to keep my mouth closed so as not to throw up. "My God, I ... I ... Oh my God, no," I whimpered. Uncle Gary put his arms around me tightly and we both cried. Looking down at her I thought over and over to myself this can't be ... It just can't be her. Her skin was a light green moss color and she was a ghostly ninety pounds. She had lost most of her beautiful hair and her lips were cracked, bloody, and pasty white. She was hooked up to several intravenous connected machines, which beeped and hummed along side her. Her eyes were sunken deep into her face and she had dark circles under her closed lids. The skin on her arms was irritated with several blood marks from her obvious fights with the intravenous needles. She looked like a sweet defenseless angel lying there with a peaceful look on her face. She looked beaten, beautiful and vulnerable. She was dying.

All I thought to myself over and over was how could God to this to us? How could he let this happen? This had to be my punishment for going to Portugal and leaving her alone. As I stood beside her bed looking down in disbelief, her eyes flickered opened.

"Where is the baby?" she asked. "Get my coat from the closet," she said. I was without words and just looked into her tired strained eyes. "It's Stephanie, Nancy. She is back from her trip," Uncle Gary said. Mom glared back at me with no response. As I stood there with my body

numb and shirt wet with the tears that had been gushing down my neck, my heart sunk. I thought to myself, she is gone. I will never forgive myself for leaving and going on that stupid trip!

"I brought you some gifts Mom," I whispered hoping the sound of my voice would bring her back to me. I gave her the box with the gold diamond ring and charm bracelet. She smiled back at me and said softly,

"I love them, thank you. Take them with you and hide them so your father doesn't find them tonight," she lay back down and closed her eyes immediately. She was asleep again within minutes.

"Let's go Steph, let's go home, we'll come back tomorrow. The medication is so strong for her the Doctors said, that it affects her brain most of the time and she can't think straight. Let's go home, we'll come back in the morning," Uncle Gary said.

"She is my home," I cried looking down at her. "She's it," I said bursting out louder, not wanting to ever leave her side again. Uncle Gary tugged on my arm towards the door. We walked out and I peered back for one last glance, hoping it would look differently from a distance. But it was just as bad as it was a second ago. My life and heart was left back in that room. She didn't recognize me and I certainly did not recognize her.

"Where's my Dad?" I asked softly as we got back on the elevator. "He's home right now, waiting for us," he replied. We walked back to my house and I felt that old familiar queasy feeling I usually felt as we turned the key and walked through the door. Portugal was now far in the rear view mirror. I was back in hell, back home. I saw the light down the hall and heard Dad sitting alone at the kitchen table, tapping nervously. As I walked through the house, my first reaction was shock. Our haunted house was now completely empty. The beds were gone, the fridge gone, the living room furniture all gone. I didn't even wonder or ask where everything was. I didn't care about any of this. All I cared about was Mom and Dad.

Dad got up and hugged me, crying loudly. Uncle Gary said he would leave us alone to talk and would be upstairs at Mami's. We both sat down at the kitchen table that stored memories of our family dinners many years ago. This time, as we sat at our old table, it was different. Everything was different. It was just the two of us sitting there, speechless. I don't remember ever sitting at the table just the two of us before that night. Dad looked thin, weathered, and tired. He had not showered for a while and his eyes were bloodshot. His lips began to quiver and I said, "I know Mom is really sick, I was just there and she is really sick."

"Yes, she has a virus. The doctor's said she had the HIV virus which has now turned into AIDS." He said not knowing exactly how to term it medically.

"AIDS?" I asked.

"What are the cures, what can she take, is there any medication she can take like chemo or something?" I went on.

"They don't know if anything can cure her. They said there are many medications they are testing but nothing can cure it. There is no cure for AIDS, at least not yet anyways, they say they are working on some which might be released soon," he explained.

I responded defiantly, "Well let's try something. They have to have some ideas on how we can get through this now?"

"We'll talk to the doctor together tomorrow. And Steph, they said I have AIDS too. I got it first and gave it to your mother. I am sorry, I did not know what I was doing and did not know she could get it too. I wanted to die but didn't want her to get it too," he began to cry again.

"I remember the night I got it, I was shooting up with this prostitute in the back seat of a car and she told me before she handed me her needle that she had the HIV virus. I didn't care and wanted to get it so I could finally die. I took her needle and used it," he said.

I said nothing, just sat there crying. He knew what he had done wrong. He knew he was sick too and that he had knowingly infected his wife, my mother. I sat there disgusted, once again, with life and with the constant pain that came our way. Was there ever going to be mercy on us? How could anyone be so reckless? How could you hurt someone else without thinking twice about it? How could life continue to beat us up? How could it just keep getting harder and harder? Would it ever just get easier?

There was nothing more that could be said that night. We both left the table and walked upstairs. We would sleep at Mami's from then on because there was no furniture left in our house. I rolled up in a ball and fell asleep on Mami's couch, trying to remember the good times we had there over the years, hoping this was all a nightmare. I tried to remember the warm sun I lay under at the beach, just a few nights ago in Portugal, and imagined myself there again.

DYING WITH AIDS

For the next few months, Mom continued to live, correction, die in the hospital. Her condition worsened every day. I practically lived in the hospital, sleeping there beside her in a cold plastic chair, as often as I could. I technically lived at Mami's and continued going to school every day. I showed up later for school some mornings and left early other afternoons. All I cared about was getting to the hospital in case Mom needed me for something. I, naively, thought she would get through this somehow. We always found a way to get by. This time it would be no different. The cure would happen right in time for her to be saved. She was in such pain that she didn't want anyone but me to help her. She said the nurses were too rough with her and would hurt her.

I fed her, helped bathe her, and gave her the pills the nurses left on her table. We watched a little T.V. together but, mostly, I watched her sleep. She lost more and more weight by the day. She had very little hair left and was somber and quiet. She was allergic to penicillin so could not take it for the pain. She was in constant, horrible, pain which was reflected in the creases in her soft face. The doctor's explained that AIDS was killing her through the gradual shutting down of every system. Her liver didn't function correctly, her lungs would fill with liquid so she couldn't breathe well, her digestive system shut down and she had constant infections. It was a horribly devastating degradation; which went on for months.

Since she was allergic to penicillin, she was given mild pain killers intravenously. Her mind had quickly slipped and she hallucinated all the time. She thought she was in danger and did not recognize anyone, sometimes not even me. During the night, she would rip out her intravenous needles and bleed all over her bed. She said they hurt her and she couldn't stand them anymore. Her soft skin around the many needles inserted in her arms and legs was blood red and scabbed. Her skin reacted viciously to any attempt to try to take away the pain. She even blistered from a face cloth, washing away the blood from her bed sores. She was so fragile and frail that everything that touched her hurt.

The doctors inserted a permanent intravenous through her neck since there was nowhere left to prick on her body. Her arms, legs, and feet were bare skin and bones; her veins had literally shriveled up. She had rashes from the sheets brushing her skin as she tossed and turned and had painful bed sores everywhere. Nanny and Mami came to visit every day. Roger, Mami's boyfriend, would come too. Dad came sometimes but couldn't bare the pain of seeing her like this. I really don't recall very many visitors because that period is all a blur to me now. My life was dying before my eyes and all I could do was give her a drink of water when she woke up and cover her feet with her blankets, trying to leave pockets of air so as not to touch her irritated skin. There was absolutely nothing I could do but watch her die, die a little more every day. My sole purpose was to make the pain a little less awful. Her lungs began to fill with liquid, so the nurses would come in to empty her lungs by inserting a vacuum type arm down her mouth. She would cry because she said it hurt so much. I could hear the crunching sound as the nurses forced the thick tube down her throat. It was as though they were cracking through her esophagus breaking off the pieces. The nurses said if they didn't do this, her lungs would fill up and she would choke to death. I eventually took on the task of emptying her lungs with the vacuum arm every hour because I couldn't bear hearing her going through the unbearable pain. The nurses were in a rush all the time because they had other patients to tend to. Handling my mother required soft caring hands. She was as delicate as a newborn baby because she had become so tiny and fragile. She needed to be touched gently and softly so as not to break her. The nurses were rough and agitated, so I began to ask them not to touch her anymore. I said I would do it. In the end, I was the only one able to touch her. I didn't want anyone to touch her anymore. They did not see the mother inside her that I did. All anyone saw was a sick woman who required a lot of attention and work. I saw my beautiful mother who was sick and needed special care.

THE NIGHT THE MUSIC
STOPPED

It was December 13 and I sat beside her as usual watching television. It was a cold winter night and it was just the two of us. I sat in my yellow plastic chair with a heavy grey wool blanket draped over me. My chair was turned at an angle facing the T.V with my back to the window. The window was frosted and I could only see the soft street lights blaring through the frost. Mom had been unconscious again for at least a week when all of a sudden, she sat right up in her bed. I jumped out of my seat and could not believe my eyes. I almost had a heart attack from the sudden movement; my heart beat frantically.

"Mom, what are you doing? How are you feeling?" I shout out quickly. "Hi, what are you doing here so late?" she asked normally. "Don't you have school tomorrow?" in her regular tone of voice that I had not heard in months. She had not been coherent for at least two, maybe three months at this point.

To hear her ask straight normal questions in Mom's normal voice was thrilling. My heart was racing as I saw a part of her that had been gone for so long.

"How are you feeling Ma?" I asked again, choking up.

"I am OK I guess. Call your Uncle Gary to come down. I want to speak with him," she said.

I immediately picked up the phone right beside her bed and paged Uncle Gary. As her condition worsened, Uncle Gary had given me a pager in case the hospital needed to contact me while I was in school. Uncle Gary also had a pager; I was told to page him if I needed him no matter what, day or night. My fingers were shaking as I entered the hospital phone number in the page. I could not believe she was awake. I hung up the phone and as we waited for Uncle Gary to call back, Mom sat back against the pillows. She had not sat up for several weeks; she was sore everywhere as she tried to move around to find a bearable position. I had tried to keep her arms and legs moving around while she was unconscious, but she was still stiff. She said she was really thirsty and asked me to give her a drink. I pulled her plastic cup close to her and gently lay the straw on her dry lips. She took a long slow sip and thanked me softly.

"Thank you Stephie, I have missed you," she whispered.

"I have been here Mom, I have been here the whole time," I responded crying softly.

"I know you have been here, I have felt you beside me the whole time sweetie," she said lovingly.

The phone rang loudly which startled both of us. The hospital was quiet at this time of night as most of the patients were asleep. I answered, "Hello, Uncle Gary? Mom is awake and said she wants to see you. Can you come now?"

He immediately responded, "I am on my way, be there in ten minutes."

I hung up the phone and sat back down on the bed beside Mom; making sure not to lean on her or sit on her.

"I have heard you beside me everyday and heard you speaking to others in the room. I have not paid attention to the other voices but always heard yours. I knew it was you touching me and taking care of me. How was your trip to Portugal? Did you love it? I am sorry I did not write more. I was just so sick and didn't know what to write. I knew you would see right through any mindless small talk. I was just so happy you were living your life and seeing the world. You were doing it for both of us. I won't ever see such a beautiful place. Thank you for going," she said smiling, with tears building up in her eyes.

She was uncomfortable propped up against her pillows. She said she just wished she could jump out of her skin; she wanted a break from the pain she felt for so long. She had become so thin and weak that she could not even lift the sheets she was so neatly tucked under. She would ask me to fluff the sheets up because her skin hurt.

"How is your father?" she asked.

I could not believe she was still concerned about him after everything she was going through. I responded back to her with a lie; intending to reassure her, "He is OK Ma, he is doing better now and is living with Mami. I am at Mami's too."

"I am sorry this is happening," she said looking right at me.

"I know you have had a horrible life these past few years and I have tried so hard to do the best I could. I don't know what I could have done differently. Maybe I could have done everything differently. But I always had you, and I was always hopeful things would get better. We always had each other and every day ran by and nothing changed. I ran out of ideas and was just scared."

I sat facing her on the bed. I did not lean on her because I would crush her legs, so I tried to balance myself on the edge of her bed. Tears were trickling down my cold face; I was looking at her thinking of how wonderful it was just to be able to talk with her again. It had been months since we had last spoken this way and it was overwhelming; almost dreamlike. I could see the pain in Mom's eyes. She no longer had that sparkle in her eyes. It had now turned to incredible sadness and pain.

Mom asked, "Did you hide the ring and bracelet you brought back for me? Can I see them, do you have them here?"

I looked at her shamefully and replied, "I did hide them Mom at the bottom of Mami's closet. But Dad found the box a couple of months ago and took it. I tried to find them at the local pawn shops but they're gone. I'm sorry."

Tears were now gushing uncontrollably down my face as I covered my face with my hands to try to hide the pain I felt. The suffering would never end. I could never forget all the tragedies and the constant torture we endured. Dad would drain us, to the very last drop, until he killed us both. When I told her the gifts I had bought her were, the sadness in Mom's eyes was overwhelming. This was the final blow she could endure.

Gary softly walked through the door just as I sat there, numb from our conversation.

He said, "Nancy! It is so nice to see you. We have missed you!"

Mom smiled and replied, "Gary, it is nice to see you again too. Thanks for getting here so quickly. I wanted to see you. I wanted to tell you that I need a favor from you. I need you to promise that you will take care of my little baby. I need you to promise you will make sure she has you looking out for her the rest of her life. I won't be here to watch her and can't leave her here alone. Make sure Richard is OK too, OK?"

"Now, now," Gary said nervously, "You're going to be around for some time, don't be foolish. It is not your time yet."

"Gary, please promise," Mom said again waiting for his serious response.

"Nancy, I will always look out for Stephanie. You never have to worry. I will take care of her as if she was my own daughter," he reassured her with a clear and convincing voice.

I just sat there at Mom's side still holding her glass hand softly. She sat back and the three of us sat silently for a while, all whimpering. Uncle Gary said he would leave us alone and would come back immediately if we needed him. I didn't move from my spot on the bed beside her because I didn't want to miss a beat.

As I sat there in the dimly lit hospital room, I knew this moment would be remembered forever. Mom still looked beautiful and stared right at me with the adoring eyes I had looked into my whole life. She always looked at me as though in awe and disbelief of the wonderful creation she had given life to. She was inspired and comforted by looking at me. She knew she had maybe come up short on many things in her life but raising me was a clear and undeniable accomplishment. She was a proud and shinning mother when she looked into my eyes. Everything she had sacrificed and endured was all worth it when she saw the potential I had and the promise for a better life.

She looked up and said, "Stephie dear, I love you more than anything, always have. You are my life and have made me happy since the day you were born. Please don't cry," and wiped my tears, barely able to lift her little hand.

"I have to die to set you free," she whispered softly.

"When I die, move far away from here and start your own life. For far too long, you have lived this life you have not chosen. Go out into the world and find your own happiness, choose your own path, live for me," she said.

Tears continued to flow into my sweater as I answered, "Mom, please don't leave me, I can't do this without you, please don't go."

She just smiled at me and we sat holding hands. She said she was tired and wanted to lie back down. I moved her pillows back and cranked the bed back down. She closed her eyes and was asleep again within a few minutes.

I sat there beside her; alone and empty again. I wanted more time; I needed more time. I had so much more to tell her. The machines all around her buzzed and purred; drowning the sound of her breathing as I was back in my plastic chair again. I sat back and pulled my wool blanket over my legs as a cold shiver ran through my body. I looked back over at her, every minute, hoping to see her eyes flicker or perhaps miraculously peer open again. But no such luck. The room had the old familiar scent of bleach and medicine that I had grown all too familiar with. I looked out the frost covered window where frozen shriveled spiders lay on the window sill. I felt like one of those frozen shriveled spiders out there. I thought to myself, how lucky are they. No more pain, no more suffering, just dead. I was only sixteen years old and felt my life was already coming to an end. I would soon shrivel up on the window sill in the snow. It was over.

I had a rickety old walkman with me in the room with a cassette from the movie "the Bodyguard." I would listen to the song "I Will Always Love You" by Whitney Houston over and over as I sat in the cold room staring at my mother. I tried to memorize the freckles on her hands, cracks in her lips and the scar on her finger from a cut she sustained while drying a drinking glass. I wanted to remember as much as I could; I knew these were the last images

I would have to hold on to for the rest of my life. Tonight, I felt my mother was closer to me since she had just come back for a brief visit. I played my song over and over with the volume turned down as softly as it would go but still allowing me to hear the music. I placed one ear phone in her ear and the other one in mine. We listened to the song over and over again together. It was my way of letting her know as she slipped far back down into the dark abyss that "I would always love her."

I spent all night watching her struggle as she took each breath. Her chest would rise less and less with every breath. Breathing looked very difficult and tiring for her. The breathing lost its usual pattern and became sporadic. It was the morning of December 14, 1992. I sat in my plastic chair still watching her breath in and out as she lingered on each breath. My walkman batteries had died during the night; the music had stopped.

At 8:34AM that morning, my mother took her last long painful breath and exhaled softly. At that exact moment in time, she let go. The same way the last note played on my walkman when the batteries finally died.

All her pain, all her fears, her disappointments, her struggles, her hopes, her dreams, her aspirations, her beliefs, her family, her love, and me was let go. She was gone. I sat there with her soft cool hand in mine. Could I hold on a little longer? How could I make this minute last forever? I immediately panicked and thought, how could I stop this from happening? I wasn't ready to let go. Should I try mouth to mouth? Should I scream at her to come back? I could never be ready to let go of her! This couldn't be it? This couldn't be the end? But then I closed my eyes and sat there still holding her hand and thought to myself "she needs to be set free." She needed to be released from the pain that had so fiercely bit its way through her. She fought a good fight and now deserved to rest. I leaned in closer and kissed her softly on her warm cheek. I took in a big breath of air to smell the scent of her soft hair and the sweet scent of her skin one last time. I was not ready to let go but knew this was not my choice. I whispered softly, "I will always love you Mom, you will continue to live inside of me till I die, many years from now. Thank you for everything you gave me."

I walked out of her room and dragged my heavy feet slowly down the hall to the nurse's booth.

I peered in and said numbly, "My Mom just took her last breath and is not breathing anymore. She is dead."

I followed the nurses back into the room and watched as one of the nurses felt for a pulse and scribbled something down on Mom's medical chart hanging from her bed. I felt lifeless; a part of me had stopped breathing too. I dared not take another look at my mother. The last glance was when I kissed her and said good-bye. That was the last memory I wanted to remember.

I was obviously still alive but felt dead inside; I didn't care about anything anymore. I called Mami and everyone spread the news amongst the family and friends. I called my school myself that morning, telling them my mother had died and I would not be back to school for a while. I don't remember where I slept the next few days or what I even did the next several months. Everything is still a blur.

TAKING MOM HOME

Mom's funeral was held in Nanny's home town of Hudson. I drove to Hudson with my father and friends, Sandra, Mary, and high school boyfriend Domenic. Michael Bolton played on the radio driving up while I sat beside Dad on the front seat. We held hands driving up as I sat numb beside him. I don't remember anything said during the funeral ceremony and I hardly remember the afternoon at the funeral home. Nanny made all the arrangements and I just sat through it all lifeless. I didn't care. I didn't care about anything, anyone, or even myself.

Nanny's friend Lillian had a son named Bernard, who was the priest at the funeral. Bernard came up to me in the funeral parlor and said, "I am sorry for your loss Stephanie, it is all over now."

I looked back at him and said faintly, "No Bernard, it's not all over. I still have to watch my father die now!"

Mom's body was so decomposed that Nanny decided on a one day wake with a closed casket. Dad and I went back behind the wake room, at the end of the day, with the funeral director for one last glance at Mom privately. The man opened the casket and I tried not to look at her face. It was not Mom. It was some strange woman lying there with loads of makeup and a dark wig on. It was a disgrace to my Mother. It looked nothing like her and was made up exactly the way my mother would have hated to be made up. I asked for a tissue and wiped off some of the heavy makeup smeared on her face. There was ugly green eye shadow and red blush smeared on her like a scary doll. Dad sobbed as I angrily tried to wipe off the nasty blubber.

"How could you guys make her up like this? It is disgusting."

I was very upset that Mom had been disgraced with the dark wig and heavy makeup. Did they not know she had been beautiful? Did my mother have to be tortured forever? How could so much pain be inflicted on just one tiny harmless person? She had never done anything wrong and had never hurt anyone. She always cared for everyone, even strangers. Why was it that the world had to crush her up until the very end?

Mom was cremated the next day and her ashes placed in a wooden box; which Nanny picked up the day after. I sat the wooden box, which held my mother's ashes, on my lap in Nanny's living room while looking out of her window to the woods. Mom and I had sat in that living room multiple times together over the years. I did not cry; just sat there frozen.

I drove back to Mami's alone, in Aunt Darlene's car, with my mother in a brown paper bag sitting in the passenger seat. I blasted the music as loud as I could and drove back crying loudly. I was pissed off at the world. I was pissed off at life and pissed off at everyone. I wanted to keep driving till I drove off the face of the earth.

I arrived at Mami's house that afternoon; waiting for me was a message on the counter, to return a phone call to a woman I had never heard of. The next morning, I called the woman from the message. It was the Women's Abuse Shelter calling me with good news. There was an opening at the shelter in Vancouver, they could accept us right away. I was stunned and furious. I could not believe the irony of the call and why God insisted on continuing to torment me.

I responded furiously, "Thanks, but my mother died yesterday. I can't believe the world we live in. A woman comes to you with her child saying they are in danger and in need of help and you tell them to wait for the call, which will come in three years. Well she's gone now and I certainly don't need you anymore. Help someone else who might still have a chance. Good-bye."

THE PIECES THAT REMAINED

My life went on, much to my dismay. God had spared me and was going to keep me alive to continue to carry these painful memories. I continued living with Mami, for a while, after the funeral. Dad was in and out of Mami's house and I didn't care about him much anymore. I was mad at the world for loosing my mother. I was mad at my father for being so selfish and giving this disease to her, mad at my mother for exposing herself and I to this hell for so many years, and mad at myself for letting all of this happen. I was mad at my family for not doing more to stop all this, mad at my friends for ignoring the obvious hell I was in, mad at God for letting me live. I felt I had been cheated. I was just mad.

Dad was not sick yet at that point. He was still on drugs and high all the time. I was barely back in school. My head and my heart were just not back in the game anymore. All I could think about were the images of my mother dying a horrible and painful death in that awful hospital. I lived upstairs from where all the hell happened and could not get any of the painful memories out of my head. I had nightmares every night and lived feeling trapped between the past and the present. I could feel my mother, still downstairs, but knew it was impossible. She was gone, I had to continually remind myself of that. It was all wishful thinking, hoping she would call me or decide to come back. But she was not going to call me. Not going to miraculously show up. She was really gone. She was gone forever. I could not believe it. I lived in denial for the longest time.

I still felt obligated to take care of my father, or at least continue to be there for him. I still felt sorry for him. Even though there was so much I wanted to yell at him, he was all I had left. I felt no one else understood the life we lived. It was now only him and I in the world left to carry on and try to pick up the pieces.

Dad moved in with a girlfriend he had made a month or so after Mom's funeral. I was not really shocked about how quickly he was able to move on since all he ever cared about was himself anyways. I really didn't care about what he did anymore. His girlfriend Paula was also a druggie and conveniently had AIDS too. They moved into an apartment in Ville St-Pierre right across the street from where my Aunt Darlene lived. I asked my Aunt Darlene if I could live with them so I could be closer to my father. She thought it was a great idea; I moved in the next day with my backpack of little belongings. Aunt Darlene did not have an enormous amount of money but ran an old folks home and had an empty room upstairs in the home. I moved into the empty room. I spent most of my time alone, listening to music. I visited my father in his apartment as much as I could bear. I could not see him when he was high but he promised he was trying to stay straight to be there for me. I was always skeptic and with reason because it was up and down all the time. I kept busy trying to finish up high school and deciding what I wanted to do with my life.

Aunt Darlene and Uncle Gary were around a lot, trying to keep the morale high by keeping Dad busy enough to stay straight. I kept to myself mostly and withdrew from the world. Aunt Darlene soon needed the room again for an old person, so I moved into the basement. I liked living there the most because my cousins Kathy and Marco's rooms were in the basement with me. I could hang out with them and not have to think about anything. Aunt Darlene's house was like a half way home during those years. My Aunt Cindy also lived there with her daughter Sherry for a while. They were down on their luck and needed a place to stay, so Aunt Darlene took them in too. Aunt Darlene was a strong woman, always caring for others. She was like Mami in so many ways, always there to take care of others in need.

Everything was a blur for so long. I tried to keep busy as much as I could all the time with work and school. I worked as a waitress in a restaurant in order to make money to pay for my own things. Aunt Darlene fed me and housed me but I had to pay for everything else myself. I had to pay for my bus pass to get to school, which was over an hour each way. I also paid for my own clothes and other items I needed. I paid for my own lunches at school too. When I was not in school or working, I spent time alone listening to music or reading. I could only think about my mother and how crappy life was. Just when I thought life couldn't get any worse, I found myself alone.

I spent time with Dad and Paula in the evenings but I didn't know if I hated her or felt sorry for her too. Now that my mother was dead, I just didn't care about anything anyways. Dad already had a girlfriend, who cared? She was a looser druggie too.

Paula had two young children of her own, which her parents were raising. More AIDS orphans was exactly what the world needed, I thought to myself. Dad would go out to get high at the slummy Motel Ideal on St-Jacques Street and call me at 2 AM to come pick him up. I was only sixteen so didn't have a car and barely had any money from my waitress job. But I would still get dressed and call a taxi. I would drive over there in the middle of the night, in the taxi, and bang on the door for my father to come out. Some prostitute would open the door and it was always a struggle to get him out of the room. The girls didn't want to let him go and I did everything I had to do to get him out of there. The next morning, I would wake up at 5 AM to catch the public bus for the long journey to school. I couldn't believe I was still bailing his butt out of all his messes after everything. My mother would kill me if she knew I was still taking care of him. I still went to the same school but now lived on the other end of town. I took two busses and two trains to get to school. I would listen to my walkman the whole way there.

I graduated from high school because the principal tutored me and I passed all the necessary tests. I was happy when to finally graduate high school and to go on to Cegep; which is Prep College in Quebec. I needed a change and was trying to figure out what exactly it was I wanted. So I figured I might as well go to Prep College and give it a try while I thought things through. I was still very depressed and had frequent thoughts of killing myself. I just didn't see the point of going on anymore. My mother was gone; killing myself would be a better alternative than living through this hell alone now. I chose to focus on the little things to get through. I took it one day at a time and thought if tomorrow is worse, I'll just kill myself tomorrow. I was hopeful that something good could maybe happen tomorrow. Besides, I figured my Dad needed me and I should stick around to at least be there for him.

Dad continued to find his way in and out of jail for theft, fighting, or possession. Wherever there was trouble, Dad found it. And I was always there to visit him during his short stays in jail and pick him up when he was released. The jail clerks came to know me on a first name basis due to my frequent visits. It was really sad having to go through the security check in order to visit Dad in jail and wait for him to come out from behind the glass. He looked so sad and ashamed. We sat facing each other, with the glass between us, trying to come up with small talk. I would try to stay positive and tell him he really needed to pull it together. I would tell him he was better than this life he was living and that I was there for him. He would promise this was the last time I would have to visit him in jail, but his words never meant much. I knew I would be back in the security line soon enough; checking in my coat and boots. I just went through the motions and took the train and bus back to Aunt Darlene's at the end of the day to prepare for my next day of school.

I made a few friends in Cegep and continued to play sports. I enjoyed spending time with friends who I felt possessed qualities that were important to learn from and eventually acquire. Since I had no parental guidance, or for that matter no guidance from anyone at all, I had to follow my own instincts. In turn, I was certain to surround myself with good people who wanted to be happy and successful in life. I shared a few classes with Cathy who was an energetic and intelligent person. We quickly became good friends and picked classes together. She did not put up with immature nonsense and had a passion for school. This was refreshing to me and I fed off her energy.

I started to live my life for myself. I kept busy at school and focused on my grades again. I studied at night, when I got home, and read on the bus ride to and from school. I knew I was at a point in my life where I had choices. I was seventeen and could only go in one of many directions. I thought of my mother constantly and could hear her words in the back of my head, "you are better than this Steph, you know it." I would imagine hearing her tell me to fight through this, that my hard work would pay off. When I found it difficult to go on, I would hear the last words she whispered to the the night she died; "I have to die to set you free." I could not betray her, the vivid memories of the pain in her eyes and the morbid smell of death in the air convinced me of that. I felt I owed my mother more than giving up. I could not take her life and death for granted. The pain and anger I felt grew into a little imaginary fire in the pit of my stomach. This fire warmed me up and gave me the energy I needed to regain my strength and think clearly. I just had to find a way to get through this. I just had to find a way to find my own life. What could make me happy?

I knew it was now my choice, my life. I figured I had two options, give up and just finally take my own life or change my life course once and for all. I did try a few half hearted attempts to take my life but soon realized that I was not being fair to Mom. She had fought so hard to keep me and raise me that I could not take my life away from her. I thought of quitting school completely and indulging in a life of drugs myself. It would torture Dad and was an appealing revenge. I would teach him a lesson he would not forget by following in his footsteps. I realized I would just hurt myself more than get even with him. He was on his way out anyways and would not be around much longer to suffer the consequences of my turning to drugs.

Finally, I realized, why not just try living a normal life for once? I had never lived a normal, quiet life. Why not try something different and see what happens? There really was nothing holding me back but myself. I had no one else to look after anymore and no one else I really needed to worry about. I did not have a little brother or sister I needed to care for so what could hold me back? I would do everything my mother had asked of me; finish Cegep, go on to graduate from McGill University, move away, and achieve a successful career doing something that would make me happy. Maybe I could afford the luxuries of life Mom and I had only dreamt of? So that was my new plan and I charged with it at full speed ahead.

I had a newly restored energy and passion but still, I took it all one day at a time. At times, my goals overwhelmed me because I put so much pressure on myself to do everything and be the best at it. I remembered the prayer Dad had learned and taught me during his rehab years:

God, grant me the serenity to accept the things I cannot change; The courage to change the things I can; And the wisdom to know the difference. When I spent time with Dad, I focused on keeping myself happy and calm.

If I did not like the situation he put me in, I just left and came back on a different day. I stopped giving him money all the time and stopped picking him up when he called me during the night. I told him he needed to take care of himself now. I think that helped him. When he realized no one was coming to get him, he eventually found a way to drag himself home. I was taking care of myself now and he would have to do the same.

My Aunt Darlene and Aunt Cindy took me to support groups a few times. I felt I was not getting anything out of it. It annoyed me to remember the hell I could not get out of. I chose to store my experiences deep down for the time being and forget it all. I stayed focused on my school work and setting new productive goals.

I graduated from Cegep with great grades and was accepted into McGill University. I had worked hard to attain these grades, so the day I received my acceptance letter, I was proud. I remember feeling proud for honoring my mother's wishes and proud of myself; pure happiness. She dreamt I would one day attend McGill University and get the education she had wanted so badly herself. Going to McGill had always been her dream and she had put it off to unfortunately never get around to it. McGill was tough to get into and tough to graduate from. The "who's who" in Canada graduated from McGill and now, little old me added my name to that list. I was proud to have graduated from McGill on my own. I paid for it myself, worked hard everyday at every class and held a full-time job while I was a full time student there. I lived my McGill experience for myself but more importantly for her. I carried two hearts inside me and felt them beat every day on campus. I would eat my lunch out in the beautiful courtyard grass looking up at the sky feeling her shine down on me smiling. She was with me every day during University.

I worked the full-time night shift at a hotel nearby and went to University during the day. The small life insurance I had inherited from my mother's clerical job, Nanny Sugrue had invested immediately in Investment Certificates which were locked for up to ten years. Nanny said not to worry, that if I ever needed money, she would give me some of hers. I was determined to support myself and spend as little as I could. The way Mom and I were forced to live for so long forced me to become frugal and extremely conservative. The money I earned at my hotel night job was enough to pay for University and the apartment I had rented. I even saved up a little on the side because I only spent on the absolute necessities to live. I did not buy any expensive clothes or go out for dinner with friends. I was too busy with a full time job and a full time school schedule to hang out with friends. I also never wanted to be poor again. I never wanted to worry about how much food I could afford in the fridge. Running out of money became a phobia of mine that I still carry to this day.

Dad was beginning to get sick, so I moved back in with Mami in our old house downtown. I wanted to stay close to him and besides it was only a few blocks away from McGill. My move was abrupt and sudden but I just needed to be close to my father and school. I was on a mission to stay focused and did not even think about the sad memories moving back into that house would conjure up. I had tucked all the memories about Mom so neatly away that I forced myself not to think about her or anything sad. I forced myself to forget about the evil house and just shut out any memories that would even try to surface. I would deal with those later. Right now, I was on a mission to succeed and could not afford a breakdown. Still, I moved into the evil house with Dad.

I biked everywhere to save money and avoid having to buy an expensive bus pass. I rode a rickety old mountain bike that Dad found in the garbage. I wasn't even embarrassed. I left the old bike unattended and unlocked outside and no one ever took it. I would bike to school and to work. I enjoyed all the biking because it kept me in great shape. I also continued to play volleyball and even played in the University Training Team. I was the shortest player on the team so knew I could not make a career out of playing volleyball, at least not at 5'6". My energy and hustle kept me on the team until I decided I did not have any time to spare anymore if I wanted to graduate early. My goal was to graduate from University as fast as I could so I could finally just move the hell out of town.

MY MOVE FAR AWAY

Dad continued to be his usual self. He was eventually too sick to go out and do drugs anymore, so he stayed at Mami's and made everyone around him miserable. He was always on his best behavior with me though. He knew I would not put up with his crap anymore and probably felt so guilty for everything that he had done that he didn't dare hurt me anymore. He was not taking care of me anymore, in fact never had. We sat and watched movies late at night and ate pizza together. Our time together was actually peaceful and nice. He was starting to get really sick but always tried to cover it up. I pretended not to notice because I did not and could not deal with it all a second time. We didn't speak much of my mother. Dad didn't talk about her and neither did anyone else from both sides of my family. Any time her name came up, everyone fell silent and sad. We never shared stories about the family we once had in the very same house; the house we all still oddly shared now with Mami. We now all lived downstairs, in the house my parents and I lived in years earlier. Mami moved downstairs soon after Mom died and rented out the top level. It eventually annoyed me that no one ever brought up Mom's name. Her name was forbidden to speak of. Everyone just chose to forget about her and take down the pictures of her in the house. Mami had many pictures of Mom, Dad, and I spread around her house along with pictures of the rest of the family. After Mom died, all those pictures were taken down. It was all very upsetting but, I guess, good for me to just avoid at that time. I was not ready to face those emotions anyways.

Dad was being treated at the same hospital as Mom. He took various pain killers and prescription drugs. He loved all the free drugs and kept saying he needed more and more to stop the pain. He would look over at me with a smirk on his face as we sat in the doctor's office and I would roll my eyes. If only the Doctor knew how much Dad loved all these free heavy drugs! The doctors had pity on Dad and kept the drugs coming.

At the beginning of my last year of University, I moved out of Mami's and into an apartment with my boyfriend Eric. I was excited about finally having my own space. We moved into an apartment in the suburbs but I was always close to Mami's. I went over after school and called every day. Dad's mind was slowly going and our conversations were becoming shorter and more upsetting. He would call me for money every day claiming he was out of cigarettes. He would yell at me if I didn't bring enough money when I came to see him.

He would say, "Don't be a bitch, gimme fifty bucks, I spent all my welfare and am out of cigarettes, don't be a bitch!"

After the hell I had forgiven him for putting my mother and myself through, I could not bear to hear him continue to yell at me and call me names. I slowly pushed him further away and he became a smaller part of my life. I moved into that apartment with Eric and for the first time had my own home. I visited Dad and Mami less frequently and cringed when he called me. He would make me feel guilty for not visiting enough and Mami would make me feel guilty for not contributing financially to help support him. The financial guilt felt the worst because I had worked so hard to buy what little I possessed and was able to save. What did they expect, I was only nineteen? He was my father, not my son! He collected on welfare, so that should be enough to buy his cigarettes and give Mami the rest for living in her house? But still they expected me to help. I just couldn't do it anymore. I just could not justify giving my father any more of my hard earned money. I made less than ten dollars an hour working at the hotel and was putting myself through school. I rebelled and stopped giving Dad any more money. I stopped listened to Mami complain about how expensive it was to look after my father. I figured they would have to figure it out on their own. I had my own bills to pay now. They always brought up Mom's little life insurance settlement and how I was lucky to get it all. I must have explained to them a million times that I didn't have any of the money and that Nanny Sugrue had locked it away in an investment for me for down the road. They must have thought I was lying and just didn't want to share it with Dad. I had only inherited ten thousand dollars from Mom's life insurance. Mami and Dad talked about it so much that they convinced themselves I was rich and had inherited ONE HUNDRED THOUSAND dollars! It drove me crazy to try to defend myself but I could never win. It is true that money drives people crazy. I just let it go and continued building my own life.

The following year, in 1998, I proudly graduated from McGill University. It had been a long and difficult struggle to finally get to this point and I had somehow miraculously pulled it all together. Once I graduated from McGill and had a College Degree, I knew I could do anything. I knew I was not condemned any longer to a life of drugs and pain. I would choose my own path, as Mom had wished. I had a few good job offers right before graduation. A few job offers were

in town and one in Toronto; which was most exciting. I loved the idea of moving away and starting in a fresh new town. I would not be running from bad memories every day and welcomed the new challenge. I accepted the job in Toronto, moved out of my apartment with Eric and prepared to move.

My McGill graduation ceremony was very nice. My friend Cathy had continued to be a big part of my life throughout my school years and we celebrated our graduation from McGill together. Dad and the whole family was there to cheer me on as I walked on stage to collect my diploma. I had endured long nights of studying and working the night shift to pay for this education and to achieve this diploma. I was proud of my accomplishment and proud of the honor it brought my father, mother, and entire family. They all knew how important this was to my mother and how hard I had worked. Everyone was there for me that night to show me they all knew where I had been and that they, too, were proud. We all went for dinner that night. At dinner I stood up and said out loud, "Thanks everyone for being here. It really means a lot to me. And most of all thanks Mom for being here. You being here with me tonight means the most. You have been with me the whole time and we finally did it." Everyone sat there in total shock and in silence. I didn't care if no one there wanted to bring her name up or remember the sad reality of her not being there to celebrate with us. I remembered her and I felt her inside me. I will always remember that day. It was a day I took a step back to stop and realize how much sacrifice was made by my mother and me to finally get somewhere good.

While I waited to move to Toronto to start my new job, I lived with Uncle Gary. I had met someone new at McGill and was serious about him. I wanted to explore this new relationship and so lived in Uncle Gary's basement for the summer while I dated Ian. Uncle Gary took me in with open arms and I could have lived there forever. He was happy to have me there and they all made every accommodation to make me feel comfortable.

I met Ian at McGill and was interested in him from the first day we met. He was very good looking and charming. He excelled in school and was intelligent. We quickly fell in love and I could see myself with him forever. After we both graduated from McGill, we continued our relationship. I accepted that job in Toronto working for General Mills and he accepted a job with IBM in Chicago.

I moved to Toronto into my Uncle Peter and Aunt Sachiko's house to begin my new career in marketing and my new life. I had finally done it. I had finally "moved" far away as my mother had wished me to. The life I lived of drugs and abuse was so far behind me now that I could barely see it in the rear view mirror anymore. Dad was comfortably being taken care of at Mami's and I was moving on with my life.

I continued my relationship with Ian and quickly moved in with him after finding a job in Chicago to join him. I was happy to start my own family and follow my own dreams. I wanted to build a normal and quiet life. I was happy with Ian and finally safe. I was excited about moving to a new city again and to live new experiences. I traveled to all these new places that I could never even have imagined as a child. I had found happiness and security. I was at peace with my place in the world for the first time.

I continued to call my father often. Our conversations were, at times, very pleasant and, at times, frustrating and disappointing. He would ask for money at the beginning and end of every conversation. Some things never changed. I tried to steer the conversation in a different direction but he would always bring money right back up. I would send him money frequently because I knew it made him happy for a whole minute and a half and besides, I had the money now. I was making good money in Chicago. I went back to Montreal often to visit. Ian's family was in Montreal as well so we both liked to go back to visit. We were always so busy visiting everyone that I spent limited time with Dad at Mami's.

As time went by, it was more and more difficult for me to walk into that old house. The evil memories that were neatly tucked away would surface as soon as I walked through the front door. They would jump out at me like a scary jack in the box. Eventually, I felt physically sick when I visited. I tried to visit as little as possible. Living far away, I forgot about the hell I had lived when I was younger. I pretended as though I was from a different place and tried to forget about all the pain. I did not think much about my father or my mother anymore. I did not think much about my old life and about Montreal at all actually. I was living in a new city and was surrounded by normal people as I concentrated on my new life. I was a completely different person now and lived in the present.

Going back home and walking through my old house knocked the wind out of me and became unbearable. The evil memories haunted my dreams for weeks after returning back to Chicago. So I stayed away.

DAD'S DUAL WITH DEATH

Dad was now in and out of the hospital and Mami was no longer able to take care of him. Dad was admitted to a long term care facility near by. I visited him a few times at that facility but mostly I called him from Chicago. He continued to ask for money in every conversation. I don't think he was aware he was asking me for money. It was probably an automatic reaction when he heard my voice, like a nervous tick. Our conversations were confusing and he was frequently incoherent. He babbled about nonsense and would then hang up. I still kept calling because I hoped maybe my voice would pull him back. Sometimes, he came back and we had a normal conversation but, many times, he yelled crazy words that didn't make sense.

Easter 2000 was just around the corner and Ian and I were planning a visit back to Montreal. I had spoken with my father and had a bad feeling that the end was near. We decided to wait till after Easter and fly up in June for our usual longer summer visit. We had just been back a few months earlier. I called Dad on Easter day and told him we were booked to come up in June for our summer vacation.

Dad said to me on the phone whimpering, "I am not good to you anymore, we don't even talk anymore, I have failed you as a father for so long, please forgive me."

I immediately responded, "Dad, you are always there for me and just being able to talk to you like this on the phone is all I ever wanted. You are a great father and I am the person I am today because of everything you and Mom taught me."

He then asked, "Do you forgive me Steph? Do you forgive me for everything?"

"Of course I forgive you Dad, I know none of it was your fault and you didn't mean for us to get hurt. I forgive you Dad and love you unconditionally, always have," I cried.

We both sat on the phone crying and telling each other we loved each other and were sorry for how everything turned out. We talked about how much we missed Mom and what a great woman she really was. We could not believe that eight years had already gone by since her death. We said we were both lucky to have had her and that she was an incredible person. I meant every word I told my father that night and truly did forgive him for the mistakes he made. I honestly felt he was human and we all make mistakes and do things we don't realize are dangerous or can hurt someone else. I also knew everything he went through and all the struggles he had faced. He tried hard to turn his life around but just didn't make it. Whatever reasons held him back from breaking through, I did not blame him for. We all make bad choices and all are weak at times in our lives. Some people's moments of weakness last a little longer than others. For Dad, his moment of weakness lasted decades.

When we hung up the phone, I told Ian that I really thought we should go up sooner. We talked about it a little but figured he would pull though as he did for so many years now and we would see him in a couple of months. Mom had been dead now for eight years and Dad was still here, so we figured he would be around for a while longer. It was tough seeing Dad live for so many years after Mom. I had sometimes thought it was a waste and wished it would have been the other way around. Mom would have done so much more with her time. She would have seen me graduate from High School, Cegep, and then McGill University! She would have seen me accept my first job offer and fall in love for the first time. She could have met my husband-to-be Ian and visited Chicago. If Mom had lived all this time, I probably never would have moved away. We would be living in Montreal and working at some great company there, living in the burbs. Mom would have continued to be a driving force in my life and would have continued to live with me all these years. I would have taken care of her and supported her.

Dad wasted all those years with the extra time he was given. He had eight bonus years to make amends with me and more importantly, to find peace with himself. I always wished he would have turned his life around for me, at least after Mom died. I wished he would have tried to be normal and live a normal life for both of us. He knew he was dying and still did nothing to mend our relationship. He did nothing to change.

On the morning of May 2, 2000 I was at the doctor's office for a checkup and received a phone call from Ian. He said softly, "Steph, your uncle Gary just called, your father just passed away, I'm sorry."

"What! What do you mean? He's dead?" I screamed as I drove back home in my car.

I pulled over and asked again, "My Dad died? I can't believe it. It can't be. We spoke last night and I told him we were coming. He said he was waiting to see me."

I was crying frantically and was hysterical. The pain was greater than I ever imagined. I thought I had already lost everything when I lost my mother but now, loosing my father, the sharp pain in my heart was back. There was so much I needed to say and so much I needed to hear from him. How could he go now? I was not ready! I sped off in my car to get home as quickly as possible, "We need to fly there now, I need to see him now Ian. Please get the tickets. I am coming home." I sobbed.

I drove home, continuing to cry frantically the entire way. When I arrived at home, Ian had packed our bags and we rushed off to the airport. I continued to cry throughout the entire trip back. The tears were gushing down my face on the plane, at the airport, and in the car ride to Mami's. I never could have imagined I would be as shocked and devastated as I was.

Uncle Gary was waiting for us, unannounced, at the airport as he had done so many times for me in the past. I smiled when I saw him and said as we hugged tightly, "I can't believe it is over. I can't believe he is gone. I don't know what I am going to do now. I had continued on all these years for my father and now?"

I had always wanted to make it easy on my father by not showing him he had ruined my life too. I pretended as though my childhood had not been so bad that I could not succeed. I fought hard to suppress the pain I felt, to live a normal life and show my father it was all OK at the end of the day. That I was OK and would still accomplish all those dreams I had told him I would as we spent hours talking on our canoe rides years earlier. Deep down, Dad was my driving force and my inspiration to continue to be strong. Now I had lost him. I knew this day would come but never planned on it. Dad was strong and would live a long time. We heard of people living with AIDS for years on television. Magic Johnson was still alive and looked really healthy. Dad would bring up Magic as an example of living with AIDS and not having any problems. So why couldn't my father continue living?

Uncle Gary just held me tightly and said, "We'll get through this, I am here for you, we'll get through this."

I asked if we could drive directly to the hospital so that I could see him. Uncle Gary said it was not a good idea because he was not himself. Uncle Gary described that my father's body had completely disintegrated and was covered in scabs and patches of blood. He bled everywhere and was literally unidentifiable.

Everyone said he looked horrible on the phone but to see it in person, words could not accurately describe, Uncle Gary continued. I agreed that I did not want to remember my father decomposed and that it would likely scar me forever. I could not take any more torture. The three of us drove to Mami's.

Mami planned the entire funeral and I followed the herds into the church, numb again. My feelings of sadness and depression were conjured up again and I remembered how painfully cruel life had been to me. The funeral was held in Lachute, where Mami was originally from. Every row in the church was full. There were hundreds of people there to remember and honor my father.

I overheard a woman whisper behind me, "She looks so much like Nancy, she is so pretty, Richard would be so proud."

Dad's casket remained closed and his picture was displayed on the casket. Right before the funeral ceremony started, I stood at the entrance to the church with the family. Aunt Darlene burst out whaling in tears. As soon as I heard her, I began to cry uncontrollably. Cousin Kathy put her arms around her mother, to calm her, and then the three of us cuddled. This was the day which would finally end the misery we all had lived for so many years. The love in that room for Dad was overwhelming and undeniable.

I stood at the podium and spoke at my father's funeral. I began sharing words about the great man that he was and how he lost his way down the wrong path somehow. I said, "His whole life he complained that he was lonely. His favorite song was actually "Just a Lonely Boy" by Elvis. He would sing that song all the time and drive my mother and I insane. He said he was always lonely and I never understood him saying that. I could never understand his feelings of loneliness when he had my mother, me, and his entire family always all around him. He was loved by so many, yet always felt so alone. We were always there to help him and did whatever we could. Dad had a passion for life and for his family. He loved everyone so much that he expected all that same love back with just as much force. My father was special. Everyone here has a story to share about my father and all the crazy, funny, happy, scary, and out of this world thing he said and did. We can all agree that he was special and that he was one in ten million. My father has made me who I am and has lit that same fire he had right here inside of me. I will carry his fire and all the greatness he was inside of me forever. He made everyone in this church today feel special at one point so let's all remember him and how special he was too."

I closed my crying eyes and stood there for a brief moment taking a deep breath. I opened them and looked at my father, his casket that is. I felt empty. I felt lonely. Suddenly, I understood how my father felt when he complained about feeling alone. I was standing there surrounded by all the people in the world that loved me, yet still felt completely alone. I realized, maybe we feel loneliness when the one person we need to be there is not. I needed my father at that exact moment and could not have that, so I felt alone. Dad had needed his father after he lost him and his father never came back. Since Dad's need was never met, he had been lonely ever since. Dad never did find his way through his loss as some of us fortunately do. I don't know what distinguishes those who can and those who can't carry on after the loss of a loved one. I don't know the secret recipe for moving on or the magical potion for coping.

All I know is some can find their way through, and others loose themselves. My father was a great man. My father was the most special man I have ever and will ever meet. Somehow though, my Dad lost his way in the mess of losing his father. He never found his way back. For that, the world lost two great men.

My mother's ashes had been sitting on Dad's dresser at Mami's these last few years. I had her urn for a while and when I moved to Toronto years earlier, I left it at Mami's with Dad. I had detached myself from those ashes because I had convinced myself that the box was not her anymore, that she was gone. I asked that her ashes be brought to Dad's funeral that day so that they could both finally be buried together. Dad was cremated as well and the two little boxes were buried in the family plot, in Lachute, on top of my grandfather's casket. We all stood there, in front of the shallow hole, and watched the two little wooden boxes be nestled into the pit. I could not grasp the reality that those little wooden boxes contained my Mom and Dad. I did not want to face the fact that both my parents were now gone forever and all that remained of their legacy was me. Crying there, in front on the pit, seemed like a weak, unsuitable, reaction. No human emotion could portray the loss I felt and still feel.

Mom and Dad's ashes lay above Papi Castagnier's casket with their names still not engraved on the tombstone. The tombstone still only reads the words written for Papi. No one knows they are buried there except for the people who witnessed the burial that day. I walked down the grassy road, back to the car, after watching the earth be shoveled back over them. I got in the car and we drove out of Lachute back to Montreal. A few days later, I was on a plane flying back home to Chicago. I have not visited their grave since that gloomy day in May 2000 nor do I have any intentions of ever visiting it.

My Mom and Dad were viciously and quickly taken from this world. They fought till the very end. They left nothing behind but me. Their legacy is the person that I am and I continue to try to be.

My life has changed in many ways since this first book. I will be releasing a sequel sharing my adventures thriving in the United States as a successful corporate banker and contestant on NBC's hit show The Apprentice! I now focus on living MY life and realizing MY dreams always carrying the memory and great energy of two incredible people - my parents. My Nanny Sugrue says it best, "Always remember who you are and where you come from. Be a real person, or a real sh*&. You decide."
Coming soon!

LESSONS LEARNED FROM DAD: LOSS, LONELINESS, COMPASSION AND CONSIDERATION

As the years have gone by, I have come to understand the feelings of loneliness my father spoke of so frequently. As I stood at Dad's funeral looking down at his casket, I realized that even though I was surrounded by all the people in the world that loved me, I still felt lonely. I needed my father at that exact moment and no one else would do. Since my father was gone and never coming back, I was overwhelmed with loneliness. Perhaps we are selfish or immature not to be able to satisfy needs with different alternatives? Perhaps our needs are basic and begin at birth? If a baby cries for her mother, no one else will satisfy but her mother. My father lost his father and was never able to overcome that loss. He was not able to find peace with that loss and move on to fill his need through happiness elsewhere. He became overwhelmed with pain and anger at the world. He lingered on the challenges he could not overcome and the upsets in his life he could not change. With this loneliness, anger inevitably formed. He felt he was alone with these feelings of anger and that no one could feel the pain he was in. The loneliness he felt inside led him to drugs and the life of abuse and self mutilation.

I have nothing but feelings of admiration, pity, disappointment, and love for my father. After everything he put my mother and I through, I can't help but to feel the loss the world has realized by losing such a great man. My father had all the potential in the world. He began with promise and ability. He was charismatic and very smart. He had the ability to lead and inspire people to achieve success. He was passionate about life and loved everyone around him. He was noble and loyal to everyone who was a part of his life. His life and death is a true example of wasted talent. His demise taught me so much about how vulnerable we all are. Even a man with such great qualities and abilities can self destruct. Man is a fragile creature, easily influenced and altered. We are easily overcome and directed by our anger and pain.

The most important lesson I have learned from watching my father's destruction is to learn self control. We are faced with temptation and decisions each and every day. The decisions and choices we make change who we are and affect those around us. We have a responsibility to ourselves and to those we love around us to do the right thing. Be compassionate and considerate. Think about how what we do will affect those we love. Being mad at yourself or not caring about doing the wrong thing could affect the ones you love the most. Think twice about everything that you do. You must realize the repercussions of your actions to those who share this life with you.

LESSONS LEARNED FROM MOM:
FIGHT FOR YOURSELF

The lessons learned from spending so much time with my mother are endless. My mother was a sweet, gentle soul who cared for everyone around her. She loved all and put everyone before herself. The most important lesson learned from my mother was, it is honorable and right to love all, but you have to love yourself first! My mother cared for my father and for me. She worried about us both and forgot what she needed. I have come to wonder, maybe if she would have thought about herself more and done more for her; it might have benefited me and my father in return? Maybe had Mom and I moved out, we could have avoided years of abuse and torture? Maybe Dad would have been forced to change if we were not around to take care of him? It is important to do what is right for you. The first step in helping those around you is to help yourself first.

There are so many maybes and hindsight is 20/20 I know. My point is that making a non-decision may be just as important as making a decision. By doing nothing, life continued as it was and eventually killed everything in sight. Sometimes, giving too much is as harmful as not giving enough. So many women think their situation is going to change. That it can't possibly get any worse. They think maybe they are not giving enough and maybe they need to try harder. What I have learned is trying is good. And continuing to try is the right thing to do. But there comes a point when it is right to move on if you are getting hurt in the process. When your life is in danger and you have tried everything you could, then you must think of yourself.

LESSONS LEARNED: TURNING FEAR INTO FIRE

Fear is all around us when we are vulnerable and hurt. I lived in constant fear most of my childhood. I feared my father would hurt us, I feared my mother would not make it through, I feared we did not have enough money to survive, I feared those around me would laugh at us if they knew how desperately poor we were, and I feared life would get the best of us. The fear inside me actually turned into a fire in the pit of my stomach and got me fighting. I fought these fears because I could not see any other way to survive. I had heard my parents praise me since birth; I just felt I was better than giving up. I felt I could not be weak and could not give in. I could not let fear take over. Instead, i decided to fight and turn this fear into fire.

I began to run faster and harder when I felt I was about to give up. I felt I owed a debt that needed to be repaid to my mother and father who had paid the ultimate price. My mother and father had fallen short. They had lost their ways and I needed to carry their torch forward. I was fortunate to have the parents that I did. They both taught me all lessons I needed to learn about life and the challenges I would face. I could not have asked for better teachers.

Mom taught me to be compassionate and honest. She taught me to be dedicated, hard working, and to persevere. She taught me to stand up for myself and not put up with anything I did not feel comfortable with. She taught me to get down to the nitty, gritty, and dirty and just get it done. To not complain about how hard work it is and just get it done.

Dad taught me to be smart and take chances. He taught me to fight for what I wanted and to take a stand. He taught me to believe in myself and that no one could do it better. He taught me that my way was just fine and would work for me. He taught me that if I fought hard enough, I could and would win. That if I was not winning then I wasn't fighting hard enough and needed to pick it up a notch. He taught me that the one who wins is the one who wants it the most. And if I wanted it the most, then I would get it.

Dad said it best when he would tell me, "Of course it is hard. Listen Steph, if it wasn't hard everyone would be doing it and you would just have more competition. Everyone who tried would be a winner and that wouldn't be right. You deserve to win because you are here, you are working the hardest and you are the best. And guess what, if you don't win, then work harder next time and it'll be yours. You can't hide behind excuses."

I would remember these words when I felt I couldn't get through. When I felt I could not pass a test I was about to take or get the job I was interviewing for. My father taught me to be passionate about life and to love everything I did. He encouraged me to go after what I wanted and to try anything. He said I had nothing to loose and my biggest regret would be not trying.

My parents were great teachers and great coaches. I almost thought they were training me for the Passion Olympics. They fed my brain all the time with passion fuel and taught me that we have nothing if we don't have that fire in the pit of our stomach. They armed me with every tool to finally have my fair chance at life and I was not going to blow it.

LESSONS LEARNED: THE DAMAGE CAUSED BY LOOKING AWAY, HUMAN RESPONSIBILITY

I was able to start a new life for myself and move "far away." I have stored all my horrible experiences neatly away and have worked hard at forgetting all the negativity I have lived. With my new life, I have come to realize that I have a responsibility to share my experiences. I have realized that my mother, father, and I felt so much pain because we felt no one was around to help. No one was around to listen, to care, or to try to help.

I have come to the realization that I have a responsibility to myself and my family to share this story. Hiding the reality of our life does no good. Talking about the mistakes we lived and sharing them might save someone else from making the same mistakes or at least let them know they are not alone. We have made those same mistakes too.

I have also come to the realization that we are all responsible for our mother, father, sister, brother, cousin, niece, nephew, friend, and neighbor. We have a human responsibility to call the police if we see a woman getting beat up in the parking lot. We also have a human responsibility to try to help someone who appears to need help. My mother and I were clearly and obviously experiencing domestic violence. Whose responsibility was it to try to help us? I used to think it was no one else's responsibility to try to talk to us because everyone had their own problems. Why should they put themselves in danger when there was nothing they could do? I have realized that the one thing that could have been done was just be a friend. If someone would have reached out to be my mother's friend maybe she could have mustered up some confidence? Or at least not felt so alone.

We are all responsible to help those we see need help. It is our responsibility to help our daughter, son, brother, sister, aunt, mother, neighbor, and friend to get up when they have fallen. Everyone has problems and we all face different obstacles, but isn't it all just a little easier when you know there is someone there if you really need them? Just knowing help is a call away makes hell just a little cooler.

LESSONS LEARNED: THE FORMS OF HELP

Help comes in many different shapes and sizes. It can be a phone call, a favor, a simple thought, a small conversation, a picture, a book, or a gesture. Help can be charity, it can be a donation, or it can be sharing time. Help to my mother would have been a friendly voice on the phone or being taken out for a friendly cup of coffee. Help to my father would have been being taken out to the movies or just hanging out with him on the couch. When you feel as though no one is there, you loose hope and purpose. My parents did not need anything more than to feel someone cared for them when they were down on their luck. They never knew what help to ask for because they couldn't even describe what they needed or how they felt. It was just sheer desperation and depression. Depression and pain is crippling. So crippling that crying out for help is impossible.

Perhaps, we all know someone who might be sitting at their frosted window admiring the luck of the frozen spider lying out in the snow? There might be someone who is lost and needs a little light shun in their direction. Let us always be aware of those around us. Help may be given to our family, friends, and passing strangers in many different forms; a smile, a helping hand, nice words, or just a little of our time.

My initial form of help is this book. Perhaps someone somewhere will read it and feel they are not alone. Know there was a girl once who lived through this mess and made it to the other side. That girl is out there and made it. If she can do it, so can you!

My second form of help is my non-profit; Child Cause / Fear to Fire Non-Profit, which can be used as a resource for information and support. Child Cause provides a peer network for teens affected by AIDS and substance abuse by inspiring them through the arts and sports. For more information visit www.childcause.com.

90

McGill University
1998

54190630R00076

Made in the USA
Columbia, SC
27 March 2019